EUROPE IN THE WORLD SYSTEM 1492-1992

Ulrich Duchrow

EUROPE IN THE WORLD SYSTEM 1492-1992

Is justice possible?

WCC Publications, Geneva

Dedicated to Philip Potter on his 70th birthday

Translated from the German by Keith Archer

Original title: *Europa im Weltsystem 1492-1992. Gibt es einen Weg der Gerechtigkeit nach 500 Jahren Raub, Unterdrückung und Geldver(m)ehrung?*, Junge Kirche, Bremen, Germany, 1991.

Cover design: Rob Lucas

ISBN 2-8254-1092-6

© 1992 WCC Publications, World Council of Churches, 150 route de Ferney, 1211 Geneva 2, Switzerland

Typeset in India by Wordmakers, Bangalore
Printed in Switzerland

Table of Contents

Introduction   vii

A Note from the Translator   x

I. Europe 1492-1992: The Changing Shape of the Capitalist World System   1
   1. The Spanish Epoch of the Sixteenth Century   3
   2. The Mercantilism (Trading Capitalism) of Competing Nation-States in the Seventeenth and Eighteenth Centuries   12
   3. The Free Trade of Industrial Capitalism under England's Leadership in the Nineteenth Century   20
   4. Fordism, Keynesianism and Neo-Liberalism in Twentieth-Century America   25
   5. Capitalism in History and the Present   38

II. The Capitalist EC Single Market 1992 – and its Consequences if we do nothing   41
   1. The Single European Market: Economic Consequences   43
   2. The Single Market and the Two-thirds World   46
   3. Division of Europe into Poor and Rich Regions   49
   4. The Fate of Farmers in the Single Market   51
   5. Social Questions in the Single Market   55
   6. The Single Market and "Sustainable Development"   60
   7. The Increasing Perversion of European Security Policy   63
   8. Reversion to Pre-democratic Conditions or Democratization of the EC's Politics and Economy?   67

III. Is Justice Possible?   71
   1. Considerations of Strategy   73
   2. Theological Considerations   78

Notes   93

Bibliography   100

Introduction

One cannot understand the contemporary period without analyzing the profound upheavals which the development of capitalism has brought about in societies throughout the world.[1]

This book is an attempt at the impossible. But the attempt is necessary, though it appears impossible in quantitative terms. How is it possible to address the question of five hundred years of Europe in the world system in such a small space and do anything like justice to it? For his monumental work *The Rise and Fall of the Great Powers: Economic Change and Military Conflict from 1500 to 2000* Paul Kennedy needed 976 pages. And here other aspects need to be dealt with as well: scientific-technological, social, ecological, political, ecclesiastical, ideological and theological.

The attempt is necessary because we are in a process of change whose direction can be understood only if we look at it in the context of past centuries. Seen this way, the history of Europe in the world system may be perceived as possessing a certain unity. Without such a perception, our understanding would be inadequate and our action blind, and we might go from one disappointment to another.

But do we *want* to see? Even without knowing all the details, we are aware that Europe has over the centuries incurred much guilt vis-a-vis other peoples and sectors of its own population. And that we ourselves are involved in this guilt in one way or another, inasmuch as we belong to those who profit from it – and that means the majority of us. That it is apt to make us defensive and suppress the past. How do we cope with it theologically and psychologically?

The question of who these thoughts are for needs to be answered. They are meant, in the first place, for the suffering, resisting losers and victims in the world system shaped by the West, in which Europe plays a central role, and for groups which try to share in their struggle and seek alternatives. Such groups – the new social movements of the civil society[2] – have come up all over the world. In Europe they are beginning to come together in various formations under the pressure of 1992, which marks both five hundred years of colonialism and resistance and the introduction of the Single European Market.

Christian groups taking part in the "Conciliar Process for Justice, Peace and the Integrity of Creation" at the European ecumenical assembly launched in Basel in 1989 the network "Kairos Europa – Towards a Europe for Justice".[3] In Greek "kairos" means "the decisive moment". In the New Testament and in Christian belief it points to the nearness of God in Jesus Christ and the Holy Spirit, and therefore to God's loving, liberating and justice-creating present. Because of it repentance and renewal are possible. The movements for justice and peace are a sign of this.

The book arises out of discussion with many of the more than two hundred groups from almost every country in Europe which are now part of "Kairos Europa". It is intended to serve as a common orientation for them.

But it is also addressed to congregations and churches in Europe. It asks them if they are prepared to accept the time of decision and turn from the worship of Mammon, and pursuits of exploitation and oppression, to faith in the suffering God of the gospel and action in solidarity with all those of every faith who, for the sake of life, seek to free themselves from the destructive structures and ethos of Western culture.

The present historical climate is not a favourable one for such a task. These groups and movements and all who long for fundamental change have in the last two years been deeply disappointed. In 1989 it still looked as though citizens' movements in Central and Eastern Europe would be able not only to overturn their own state-capitalist, bureaucratic systems, but also to stimulate more democratic, economically just alternatives in the West. But the forces of change in the former German Democratic Republic have again been marginalized, and the gap between rich and poor in the West has become even more pronounced. The countries of Eastern Europe are suffering from economic collapse because of their burden of debt, world market conditions, and their own disintegration. The Gulf war made it clear that, despite the growing peace movement and the desire throughout the world that resources be diverted from arms to development, the capitalist US and its allies are as intent as ever on going ahead with their policy of imperialism and militarism. Similarly, the stubborn resistance and development work of the majority of the Nicaraguan people and the international solidarity movement failed in the face of American Low Intensity Conflict.[4] The freedom struggle in South Africa is threatened with the same fate. Only the long-drawn-out efforts of the Namibian freedom movement and its allies have led to success and political independence.

Given this situation there is a danger of widespread hopelessness. It can take various forms: some people conform; others turn to activism; yet others seek comfort in drugs of various types, including certain kinds of religiosity; those in power strengthen their positions. This makes sober analysis and intensive discussion on strategies for resistance and change all the more necessary.

A book like this can of course make no claim to be complete or to cover all the issues. It can only present a possible framework for action and hope to stimulate people to further work on their own.

A Note from the Translator

Readers used to the writings of Ulrich Duchrow will have come to expect of him a stimulating blend of history, economics and theology, synthesized in a way that is both challenging and intellectually and spiritually nourishing. This little book will not disappoint them.

But writers write in and out of a particular context, and their readers very often read and interpret them in terms of another. This is clearer than ever when translation intervenes between the writer and his readers. Although as translator I hope it will not be obvious that a German original lies behind my English style, Duchrow's German *context* cannot be disguised. Nor should it be. If English-speaking readers find references to German history or the present German scene which are unfamiliar, let them be patient. For in many ways Duchrow's German, Central European perspective is of positive value – particularly if the reader happens, like me, to be British.

Naturally, we all regard the world as if our little bit of it were its centre. Duchrow, therefore, challenges me to look at the world not as it appears from the British Isles but from the heart of the European continent. That sets British (and American) history in the wider context of Europe's dealings with the rest of the world over the last five hundred years. Salutary as that is, I find it even more important that Duchrow invites me to see the European Community from a perspective that does not come naturally to me.

In our heads we all know that the EC is here to stay, but in our hearts it seems less clear. Most British debate over the EC still seems to hang upon the unstated but implicit question: Do we really want to be part of it at all? Or would we rather either go it alone or entrust our future to closer links with the USA?

As a German, Duchrow's approach to the EC is very different. His country's history and geography set him firmly within it. But that does not make him uncritical of it. Quite the opposite. Accepting it as a fact of his country's politics, he is able to analyze it as he does the German scene or others their own. So whilst the typical British stance tends to make somebody like me a mere spectator of the EC policy game (remember Mr

Major's "triumph" at Maastricht!), Duchrow urges the need to get in there and go for it. For his analysis reveals a window of opportunity. Many of the EC's obvious imperfections stem from its essentially capitalist origins, he argues. Some, however, are because its institutions are still fluid, still in a process of change. This makes them unusually open to pressure, and at least potentially responsive to the cries of the victims of injustice.

Duchrow's analysis therefore gives grounds for neither resignation nor despair, despite the evils bequeathed to the world by five hundred years of European history. Rather, it is a call to hopeful action.

Keith Archer
Manchester, England

Part I

*Europe 1492-1992:
The Changing Shape of the
Capitalist World System*

1. The Spanish Epoch of the Sixteenth Century
2. The Mercantilism (Trading Capitalism) of Competing Nation States in the Seventeenth and Eighteenth Centuries
3. The Free Trade of Industrial Capitalism under England's Leadership in the Nineteenth Century
4. Fordism, Keynesianism and Neo-Liberalism in Twentieth-Century America
5. Capitalism in History and the Present

Thesis 1

With the conquest of America from 1492 on, modern history begins as a world history defined by Europe. It is characterized by the capitalist system, which takes different shapes as different subjects follow the basic principle of utilizing capital to achieve profit. The main actors are banking, trading and industrial companies which, with changing political and social allies in Europe (and later in the US and Japan as well), build centres of power with the help of which the whole world is increasingly made capitalist. Knowledge of the capitalist world system and also of the resistance to it is indispensable for responsible action today.

What is the point of marking these five hundred years? To act meaningfully, is it not sufficient to analyze the present world system and define our place in it?

If there is one thing characteristic of the capitalist system in which we live, it is its flexibility and ability to change and adapt to altered circumstances. Although Karl Marx and the theories based on his thought considered that the crises capitalism produces would lead naturally to its downfall, since the collapse of "real socialism" this assumption has finally been disproved. Capitalism has shown a continuing capacity to survive crises, though whether nature and the greater part of the world population will survive with it is another question. A look at the five-hundred-year history of the capitalist world system that came out of Europe can help us understand capitalism's core, the way it changes, and its present form and development. This is important for drawing up a strategy for achieving ecological and social goals in and against "real capitalism".[1]

It is equally important to be aware of the ideological legitimations with which this system was justified. For the most part they are still used today. The role of churches, missions and theologies has also been significant. Finally, we can learn from the success and failure of forms of resistance in earlier centuries.

1. The Spanish Epoch of the Sixteenth Century

> Thus I say of these Indians, that these mines, treasures and riches were a means of their predestination and redemption; for we see clearly that, wherever they are, the gospel comes in plenty and with eagerness. Yet where there are none, just poor people, this is a means of rejection, for there the gospel never goes, since, as experience abundantly teaches, no soldier or general will go to a land without this endowment of gold and silver, and also no preacher of the gospel.[2]

> The sole and true root cause why the Christians murdered and destroyed such an enormous mass of guiltless people was simply this, that they sought to take into their power their gold. Their wish was to enrich themselves with

treasures in a few days and thus to rise higher than their station and connections allowed.[3]

It happened that a chieftain called all his people together. Each should bring whatever gold he had, and all of it should be placed together. And he said to his Indians: Come, friends, this is the god of the Christians. For we will dance before it for a while, then go to the sea and throw it in. When they find that we no longer have their god, they will leave us in peace.[4]

The cazique (on a pyre in Cuba)... asked the priests whether Christians went to heaven too. Certainly, said the priests, all good Christians go there! Immediately and without thinking the cazique replied that he would not wish to go there, but rather to hell, lest he should see more only the same cruel people, nor have to stay where they were.[5]

Thesis 2

In the capitalist world system's first phase the kings of Spain and Portugal, and later the Hapsburg emperors, use the capital-owning houses and city-states of Upper Italy and Upper Germany in order to amass enormous wealth. In the process agriculture is capitalized, the arms industry assumes precedence, the population is impoverished, crown and nobility get into debt through high living and wars, the conquered territories are robbed of precious metals and raw materials with the aid of fire-arms and slavery, and 90 percent of their inhabitants are killed in the greatest genocide in world history. Pope Alexander VI acts as Supreme Liege Lord for the Spanish and Portuguese Conquistadores. A theology of slavery legitimizes the position of colonialists and capitalists, a state theology legitimizes the royal tribute system, liberation theologians like Las Casas fight on the side of the original inhabitants.

Robbery and murder of the peoples of America, Africa and Asia is the basis of Europe's wealth and world leadership. There is a mass of literature on the subject, and the angle from which the books are written is important. School text-books usually narrate these events from the Eurocentric viewpoint of the victors; it smoothes the rough edges. Thus we read of the "discovery of America", not the conquest and plundering of this continent. The monumental work by Kennedy which I have already mentioned devotes to the whole question of "cruelty" three sentences – and these in order to justify it.[6] But there are also books written from the viewpoint of the victims and of resistance. I shall deal with some of them here.

Written with particular clarity and detail is Fernando Mires's book *In the Name of the Cross. Genocide against the Indians during the Spanish Conquest: Theological and Political Discussions.*[7] We have always assumed that the main actors were the kingdoms of Spain and Portugal. But Mires shows that they were only "junior partners", even instruments of the capital-owning families of, above all, Upper Italy and Upper Germany which with their help concentrated on money-making (accumulation of capital) through universal expansion. The riches stolen from Latin America ended up mainly in their treasuries:

> The money produced its own specific traders: small speculators, who hung around the gates of palaces and even pushed their way into the monasteries. The nobles and the prelates wrapped themselves in silk; yet they had no idea how, when they had dressed in their finery, they might pay their debts. Even the crown got itself way out of its depth in debt. Even ministers could not understand this fateful development: the more gold flowed into the country from America, the poorer the country became and the more it ended up in the hands of the bankers, who were once so despised but who showed themselves more and more to be the real rulers of Europe.[8]

Their first big growth phase was in the twelfth century. Then the popes appealed for sacrifices for the *crusades* against Islam, and gigantic sums of money flowed into Italy, and thus into the banking houses of Venice, Florence, Genoa and Milan.[9] They lent the money for armies which had to be supplied with the equipment they needed before sailing from Venice,[10] they strengthened the Mediterranean trade as far as India in order to provide Europe with luxury goods such as fine silks and spices. Money-making and military expansionism linked with the belief that Christianity was superior to any other religion was the mixture out of which the crusades were made. And it is exactly this mixture that determined European and later Western world domination. The influence of the crusades on European and world history cannot be overestimated.[11]

This was the state of affairs at the dawn of the year 1492. The transnational banking and trading houses were able to motivate the Spanish nobility to expel their competitors, the Jewish and Muslim merchants, from Spain[12] – one of the reasons why the country was not able to use the stolen wealth productively. After this "reconquest" of Spain the banking houses financed the wars of conquest (Conquista) against the original inhabitants of America. Soon there were the gold and silver mines worked by slaves and the new coffee and sugar plantations to exploit the fast-growing trends in consumerism, and then the attempt by the house of Hapsburg to make the whole of Europe its empire.

Thus came into prominence the Augsburg house of Fugger, which in 1525 bought votes for Charles V's election as emperor. The Welsers and the Fuggers had taken into their direct ownership whole regions in Latin America, the latter in present-day Venezuela, the former in Chile.[13] Las Casas writes of these "German merchants":

> ...they raged much more cruelly [at the Indians] under them than all the barbarians I have already mentioned [i.e. the Spaniards]; more bestially and furiously than the bloodiest tigers and the angriest wolves and lions. In their avarice and greed they were much more frantic and deluded than all those who came before, they devised even more abominable ways of extorting gold and silver, they set aside all fear of God and the king and all shame before men; and

since they enjoyed such great liberties and held in their hand jurisdiction over the whole land, they almost forgot that they were mortals.[14]

But it would be quite wrong to regard these as the evil acts of morally culpable and particularly covetous individuals. In the early modern period the new structures of a world economy developed which, as a capitalized money economy, reached increasingly into all areas of life.

When I speak of actors, I mean social groups in interaction with certain structures and institutions and also basic cultural conditions. Aristotle observed that money, apart from its function as a means of exchange for trade between the producers of necessary goods, lends itself to being used to increase wealth directly (profit through interest and trade).[15] In this "dual economy" increasing wealth was related above all to warfare, the international trade in luxury goods, and mining for precious metals and coin-making. Now, however, its influence spread to ever more vital areas of society and it was a decisive factor in the emerging European world system.

The first area is agriculture. Immanuel Wallerstein wrote the key work on this: *The Modern World-System: Capitalist Agriculture and the Origins of the European World-Economy in the Sixteenth Century* (1974). He sums up the state of the preceding feudal system as follows:

> What we should envisage, then, when we speak of Western European feudalism, is a series of tiny economic nodules whose population and productivity were slowly increasing, and in which the legal mechanisms ensured that the bulk of the surplus went to the landlords who had noble status and control of the juridical machinery. Since much of this surplus was in kind, it was of little benefit unless it could be sold. Towns grew up, supporting artisans who bought the surplus and exchanged it for their products. A merchant class came from two sources: on the one hand, agents of the landlords who sometimes became independent, as well as intermediate size peasants who retained enough surplus after payments to the lord to sell it on the market; on the other hand, resident agents of long-distance merchants (based often in northern Italian city-states and later in the Hanseatic cities) who capitalized on poor communications and hence high disparities of prices from one area to another, especially when certain areas suffered natural calamities.[16]

The growth of agricultural productivity in the Middle Ages was due mainly to a technological revolution, whose elements came largely from the non-European cultures of the Near and Far East: better ploughing techniques, three-field husbandry, the yoke for harnessing horses, and the water-mill. The combination of these techniques resulted in a significant increase in agricultural production. A not unimportant factor was the collective way of working and the education work of the Benedictines and later the Cistercians.

As long as this growing agricultural surplus was only partly translated into the consumption of luxury goods and warfare by the nobility and increased wealth for the merchants, Europe prospered, which led to an astonishing population growth. But about the middle of the fourteenth century there was a serious crisis, for which the following factors were responsible.[17]

• *Agriculture* became dependent on owners of capital in the cities as the economy was increasingly monetarized, and it suffered under the rising taxation of the emerging nation-states, waging war among one another and in the colonial territories. The peasants responded through a series of peasants' wars. Only the Swiss Community of Oaths succeeded in organizing itself independently, since this took place before the development of firearms.[18] All the other peasants' revolts were ruthlessly suppressed, in Germany finally in the Peasants' War of 1525.

• But not all those in the cities were winners. An *urban proletariat* of wage-labourers emerged, to begin with mainly in textile production. Owing to many factors, including the invention of the flywheel, they were forced into a work process geared to profit.[19] At the same time, all independent workers, because of the "price revolution" of the sixteenth century (related to inflation), had to accept a reduction in real wages.[20] Here too the revolt of the Florentine textile workers, the Ciompi, as early as 1378, showed that people did not accept new forms of exploitation by the owners of capital without resistance.[21]

• A decisive technological invention which had drastic consequences for Europe and the whole world was the *fire-arm*. Karl Georg Zinn has explored its significance in an exciting book, *Cannons and Plague: On the Origins of the Modern Period in the 14th and 15th Century*. Through this invention the arms industry became the driving force of urban technological development.[22] For with it, big profits could be made very fast. Above all it enabled the conquest of large tracts of land at relatively low cost and even the subjugation of great empires whose leaders did not have this weapon. Pizarro's conquest of the Inca kingdom in Peru and Cortes's subjugation of the Aztecs in Mexico – with a mere handful of adventurers – are the best known of many sad examples.

• Why were Europeans prepared to use these new weapons of mass destruction with such *brutality*? After all, the China of the Ming period had already invented gunpowder and at the end of the fourteenth century had used fire-arms against the Mongols.[23] The Chinese also made major expeditions along the coasts of South-East Asia and East Africa. But they never murdered and plundered as the Europeans did.[24] Zinn[25] draws attention to the role which the great waves of plague in Europe might have played in this. About a third to a half of the European population perished in the Black Death after Genoese galleys brought the epidemic from the Black Sea in 1347. In response, people not only tried to keep strangers at a distance but also looked for scapegoats among minorities. The main victims were the Jews, who were accused of "well-poisoning". The first systematic pogroms were launched in the first wave of the plague.[26] Zinn says in summary:

The psychopathological phenomena of the fourteenth century may be explained in terms of a growing intensity of deprivation [fear of loss]. Aggression was directed at groups that were traditionally exposed to discrimination already. Pogroms and other related manifestations of the plague period like un-Christian mass burials, the rejection of sick neighbours and relatives, fleeing the epidemic in spite of duty, etc., added to the widespread subjective guilt feelings ("God's punishment") objective grounds for guilt. They were collectively displaced, and came out, as we know today, in aggressiveness in society.[27]

Zinn considers the links between brutality and civilization,[28] and speaks of the "aestheticizing of the terrible". We know of the German concentration camp torturer who is a good father and a music lover at home. Even the refinement of eating habits, with individual knives, forks and table placings at such a gregarious occasion as a common meal, could be a sign of the greater distance and aggression between people as a result of the plague. The trial of witches is a further indication of the "civilized" destruction of people.[29] In the face of epidemic and war people looked for new survival strategies. "They found them in the more egoistic, more socially inconsiderate behaviour which crystallized in the 'civilized' competitive behaviour of market societies."[30] In Europe, and even more in their dealings with subjugated peoples in the colonies, the ruling élites of the modern period conducted their struggle for dominion with the brutal violence of fire-arms, which were a means of mass destruction. Galtung has pointed out rightly that the atrocities of fascism were simply the application of methods used against other peoples to parts of the European population; thus "Marxism is Western civilization *in extremis*". "Nazism in particular and fascism in general are a phenomenon that comes into being when capitalism is in crisis and is no longer capable of operating (meaning giving adequate return for investment) smoothly or softly."[31]

• Weapons technology and this deeply-rooted distance from and brutality towards fellow creatures help to explain another feature of modern Europe: Europeans' inability to understand "the others" on their own terms. Tzvetan Todorov has pointed to this in his book *The Conquest of America – The Problem of the Others*.[32]

• Franz Hinkelammert goes even deeper into the analysis in his book *The Faith of Abraham and Western Oedipus: Sacrificial Myths in the Christian West* (1989). Instead of rejecting child-sacrifice as in the story of Abraham's aborted sacrifice of Isaac (Gen. 22:19), the West follows the Oedipus myth, in which Iphigenia makes a voluntary sacrifice to the father's *law*. This expresses the absolutizing of rulership. Through the Christianization of the Roman empire Christian freedom is identified with the law of the ruler. Anselm of Canterbury introduced this idea into the teaching about God: God's justice is expressed in the fact that, because guilt must be paid for, he must sacrifice his Son. Thus – quite differently from the biblical tradition in which God is experienced as a loving, life-protecting power – law is set above God. It is the most perverse inversion of the biblical message of liberation when it becomes an order, a law, a structure claimed to be valid now and imposed through violence against life – whether it manifests itself as an imperial power in Europe or the colonial territories, the free market, bureaucratic-socialist planning, or even the church as an institution. From this perversion grew, with cross and sword, the crusades and the Conquista.

• This brings us to the role of the *church* and *theology* in the development of the world system shaped by Europe. In 1492, the "discovery" of America and its riches was seen in Spain as God's reward for the ejection of the Jews and Muslims, the Reconquista (later also as a compensation for the loss of territories to Protestantism). Columbus understood his quest for gold as a means of financing the eventual reconquest of Jerusalem.[33] Thus we see that the conquest of America was directly linked with the imperial tradition of the crusades: crucify the crucifiers! When we go into details we can identify at least three different positions within the church, corresponding to the interests of the different social groups: those of the colonialists, the state and the Indians, as Mires and Gutiérrez in particular have shown.

First, in the early Conquista period the war against the Indians was based on the need to convert them.[34] When the king "assigned" land and Indians (Repartimientos) to the conquerors and entrusted them with evangelization (Encomienda), they converted the gift into a capitalist slave trade.[35] Since there was in Spain no theological basis for *slavery*, one was developed from the following arguments: "the Indios are by nature of less worth"; "the sins of the Indios must be punished"; "even before the Conquista the Indios lived under an unjust rule"; "the Conquista is a necessary evil".[36]

The notorious Juan Ginés de Sepúlveda, Las Casas' great opponent, went even further; he was the first great ideologist of slavery and capitalism.[37] He "derived civil law directly from the rules of war and thus established violence as the source of law".[38] He justified himself by blaming nature, from which wars inevitably come. The Christian attitude of non-violence was only for the heart, and not applicable to society and politics: a modern version of the so-called Two-Kingdoms teaching. War was allowed by natural law for: (1) defence against violence; (2) reappropriation of stolen property; (3) punishment of criminals. From Aristotelian natural law de Sepúlveda also deduced human inequality: "Thus the man rules over the woman, the adult over the child, the father over his children, i.e. the more perfect and powerful over the less perfect and the weak."[39] The connection with paternalism, racism and colonialism is obvious. It is characteristic, finally, that one of his "proofs" of the "natural" inferiority of the Indios is that Indian societies are not organized on the basis of private property.[40] Private property also became a criterion for distinguishing between civilization and slavery – an argument we shall encounter again with John Locke.

Second, we find alongside this open, radical position of a capitalism based on natural law, bellicose and dependent on slavery, the position of the state and the official church. This is not identical with the first position, and is indeed even critical of it. For the tendency of the Conquistadores and colonialists (Encomenderos) to assume completely autonomous direct power over land and slaves collided with the crown's interest in maintaining sovereignty and taxation rights over the new territories. It therefore favoured a direct *tribute system* and consequently a form of "separate development" in which the Indios lived in closed communities and paid tribute. So the church and the orders helped with the development of so-called reductions. Mires calls this the "centrist" or middle position.[41] It is further strengthened by one of the fathers of modern civil law, Francisco de Vitoria.[42] For him the Indios are both individuals and subjects of civil law. Therefore they are to be recognized as owners of property. Yet even he makes no radical rejection of the wars against the Indios.

Third, we find in the church, above all among the religious, the *indigenist position* of an active minority, whose best-known representative is Bartolomé de Las Casas.[43] As a cleric Las Casas himself had been leader of the Encomenderos in Hispaniola (today Haiti and the Dominican Republic). In 1514 a Dominican father refused him absolution and communion because he had not fulfilled his duties towards the Indians.[44] Then at Pentecost – as he himself reports – he was meditating on some biblical texts, among them Ecclesiasticus 34:18-22:

> A sacrifice derived from ill-gotten gains is contaminated,
> a lawless mockery that cannot win approval.
> The Most High is not pleased with the offering of the godless,
> nor do endless sacrifices win his forgiveness.
> To offer a sacrifice from the possessions of the poor
> is like killing a son before his father's eyes.
> Bread is life to the destitute,
> and it is murder to deprive them of it.
> To rob your neighbour of his livelihood is to kill him,
> and the man who cheats a worker of his wages sheds blood.

He became convinced that all the crimes mentioned here were committed out of greed for gold in the West Indies – reason enough "to think about the misery and the slavery which those people have to endure". He was converted and became the great defender of the Indians for the rest of his life.

• He formulated the decisive theological question: God or gold, the God of life and liberation or the death-dealing god of money?

• He did not restrict himself to works of charity, but he attacked the structural sin of the war against the Indios and the Encomenderos capitalist slave system in the mines and plantations. Here Las Casas came across Luther's fundamental rejection of the emerging capitalist system and his observation that, with its total concentration on money-making, it was fundamentally a violation of the first commandment. It is worship of the "idol" mammon.[45]

• He sought alternatives in the form of independent settlements for the Indios.

• He appealed incessantly to those with political responsibility – in this case, the king and the emperor – to try and remove the Encomenderos system of economy, guarantee that wrongs would be corrected, and enact laws for the protection of the Indios – with great success, as in particular the Leyes Nuevas show. In this he skilfully exploited the opposing interests of the crown and the colonialists. His arguments, as unfolded by Mires and Gutiérrez, are an arsenal for the theological, economic and political struggle for resistance against and liberation from the capitalist-colonialist system right up to today, even if he did not achieve all his goals in his own time.

So these are some of the factors in the change to the Europe-determined, capitalist world system – economic, technological, political, mental, theological and ecclesiastical. There are many more, and of course some are more important than others.[46] Crucial is the interplay between them, and the question of how the rising ruling class of capital-owners made use of them and what strategies of resistance were developed by their victims.

And here we have the key to understanding the transition from the Spanish period to the next phase, mercantilism.

As we have seen, the banking and commercial houses of Upper Italy and Upper Germany had focused on the imperial house of Hapsburg as a political and military support for their pursuit of profit. But their attempt to unite Europe and the colonies into a classical empire had failed. There are two main reasons for this: (1) The military cost of extending this empire within and outside Europe and defending it exceeded its economic capacity, chiefly because the banking houses had to be paid enormous profits in interest on their loans. So the empire "overstretched" itself – which, according to Kennedy's theory, is the main reason for the decline of great powers.[47] Along with the empire, the power of the Fuggers and the other banking houses also collapsed. (2) The basic weakness of the Spanish economy lay from the beginning in the fact that the enormous riches stolen from the colonies were spent lavishly, not just on more warfare but also on consumption of luxury goods by the nobles and the church. Part of the gold stolen from the Incas, for example, may still be admired today in the impressive ceiling of Santa Maria Maggiore, ten minutes from the station in Rome. Such stolen wealth was not invested in productive economic areas like agriculture and industry.[48]

This was precisely what the owners of capital in the city-states of North-West Europe and the newly emerging territorial nation-states like Holland and England did, thus laying the foundations for the mercantilism which followed.

2. The Mercantilism of Competing Nation-States in the Seventeenth and Eighteenth Centuries

With the failure of empire, the bourgeoisies of Europe realized that their economic and social future was tied to the core-states.[49]

Thesis 3

The trading-capitalist phase of mercantilism in the seventeenth and eighteenth centuries is characterized by monopolistic trading companies, supported by strong, centrally organized nation-states – above all Holland, England and France. The free Hanseatic cities of Northern Europe play a secondary role. These trading companies organized the infamous triangular trade: with technology stolen from India in particular, finished goods are produced in Europe (textiles, above all). These and weapons, alcohol and trinkets are sold in Africa for profit, and with it African people are bought. The human cargoes are taken in the same ships to the Caribbean and America and those who survive the hellish crossing are sold as slaves on the plantations there, again at a profit. As well as precious metals, sugar, cotton and other raw materials are bought and then resold with further profits in Europe, where – particularly in ports like Liverpool – enormous capital sums are accumulated to keep this circulation process in motion.

The ideological basis for this state-supported money-making economy comes from philosophers such as Thomas Hobbes, and John Locke who becomes the father of Western state constitutions. In this phase the Protestant churches begin to set up missionary societies analogous to trading companies. Theologically the dam of the prohibition of usury is broken, and only small minorities pursue the struggle against slavery.

But there are also examples of resistance and alternative thinking in this period: the Jesuit state in Paraguay, the Indian communities stimulated by John Eliot in New England, and the self-liberation of the slaves in Haiti under Toussaint Louverture.

I wish I could say, following Max Weber, that capitalism has a special affinity with Protestantism, and particularly with the doctrine of Election, the work ethic, thrift and Calvinist rationality, and that it was therefore particularly in Holland and England – and to a lesser extent (because of the Counter-Reformation) in France as well – that the most intensive development of this form of economy and society took place during the mercantile phase. The coincidence of the ideological and religious division of Europe with the shift of political and economic power from Southern to Northern Europe is indeed striking. However, Herbert Lüthi has demonstrated not only that Weber's theory is built on far too narrow an empirical basis, but also that all the elements of capitalism existed before Calvinism. Their rejection in the course of the Counter-Reformation, which favoured the old powers and ruling groups in society, merely brought "modern" forces together in the Protestant countries, where interaction with clearly Protestant attitudes strengthened their economic effect.[50]

A more significant factor in the shift of political and economic power in Europe is surely the growth of strong, centralized states, able to support and protect the property accumulation of the mercantile classes. Wallerstein's basic thesis is "that three things were essential to the establishment of such a capitalist world economy: an expansion of the geographical size of the world in question, the development of variegated methods of labour control for different products and different zones of the world economy, and the creation of relatively strong state machineries in what would become the core-states of this capitalist world economy".[51] We considered the expansion in detail in the last section. We shall now concern ourselves particularly with slavery as a method of controlling work. But first let us look at the development of state machineries.

It is worthy of note that the political and economic powers which led the way earlier did not make the decisive leap to the centre of European power but declined on the "semi-periphery". That was because they were unable to build up an effective centralized bureaucracy to support their economic power — Spain, as I have shown, was overstretched by the dispersed empire, and neither Italy nor Germany at that time achieved the national unity which in England and France enabled the centralization and strengthening of an effective administration.

Why, then, was Holland, first of all, able to play such a central role?[52] The Low Countries (General States) had been rebelling more and more against the overlordship of Spain since 1566, because of the increasingly heavy tax burden and its attempts at re-Catholicization. The result was a division that could no longer be ignored into a Protestant North and a Catholic South. The North became a republic with the merchants as its strongest class — the result, in effect, of a first bourgeois revolution. This made it possible to strengthen the administration to the maximum benefit of mercantile interests without the over-centralization of the monarchies.

Of course, the main reason why Holland played such an important role between the periods of the hegemony of Spain and England was economic. During a recessional phase Amsterdam controlled the grain trade with the Baltic states. The important trade in wood for building was also based there, which gave rise to a booming ship-building industry (and the production of a number of finished goods), which in turn strengthened Holland's share in the Atlantic trade. Pirate raids on Spanish freighters, laden with precious metals from the New World, were also profitable. Moreover, Holland took over from Portugal control of the Asian spice trade. After Antwerp which, with North Italy and the Fuggers, had been the most important financial centre in the Hapsburg empire, fell along with Southern Flanders to Spain and in its decline was pulled down with it, Amsterdam took over the leading role in the European money business as well. Militarily Holland was sufficiently well equipped to be able to hold its own among the neighbouring great powers.

Of these, England and France were the strongest and most centrally-governed nation-states of the late seventeenth and the eighteenth century.[53] Organized on a strictly mercantile basis, they waged economic and military wars in Europe and on the colonial world market until finally England, after the Battle of Waterloo in 1815 in which Napoleon was defeated, emerged as the undisputed victor and the hegemonic power of the nineteenth century.

Let us concentrate on the example of England.[54] There were several factors that contributed to England's ascent. In the fifteenth century textile manufacture had developed as a secondary means of income in country areas. The cloth was not of high quality, but it was produced in increasing quantities, which meant England had to find export markets.[55]

Between 1530 and 1542 the country had already developed an effective centralized administration.[56] Because of a relatively long period of internal peace in the sixteenth and early seventeenth centuries and her island situation, England had no standing army, and military expenditure was lower than among the warring continental powers. Since in the Reformation under Henry VIII the state had appropriated church and monastery lands and sold them, farming was capitalized, and there arose in the process an aspiring landowner class in the form of the gentry and yeomenry, who produced for the market and added value. Together with the merchants they formed the rising bourgeoisie, which emerged as the final victor out of the civil war of Cromwell's English revolution in the mid-seventeenth century – although to all appearances the crown had won.[57]

With the Enclosure of land for pasture (for the production of wool for the textile industry) many peasants lost their land and the population was impoverished, which led to vagrancy, migration to the towns and a reservoir of cheap labour. Finally, through the fleet's superiority over the Spanish Armada in 1588, England was able to carve up the declining Spanish empire. For a long time English ships had attacked Spanish ones with their cargo of stolen precious metals, and this pirate booty greatly increased England's resources. Now Cromwell was able to conquer Jamaica in the Caribbean. Also – in increasing competition with the Dutch – the Portuguese monopoly of the spice trade with India was broken.

The world market itself was organized along a pattern of *Triangular Trade*. E. Meueler provides a useful explanation for it in his textbook on "Underdevelopment".[58]

Changing Shape of the Capitalist World System 15

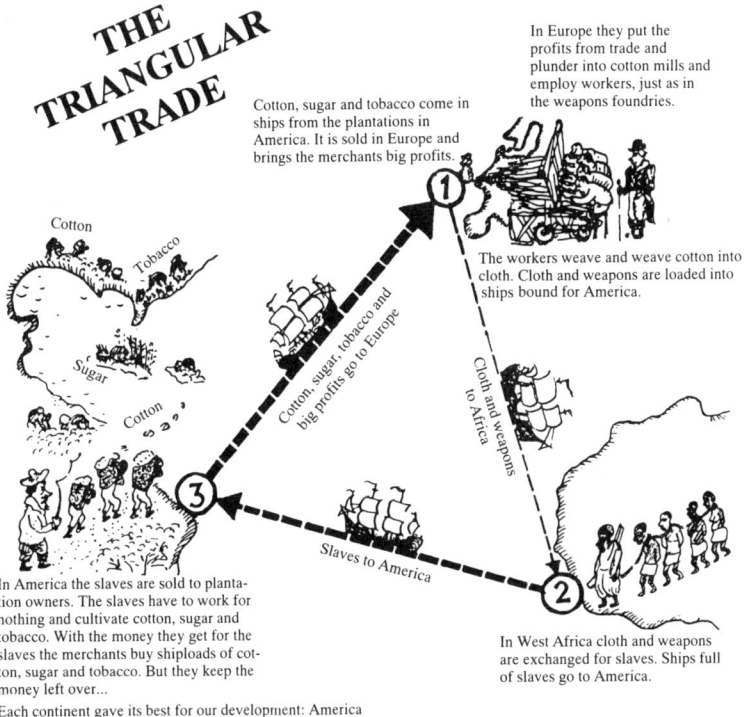

Each continent gave its best for our development: America gave gold, India art and technology, Africa living people. Who can ever forget their suffering at our hands?

The biggest state-protected trading companies with a monopoly were the Dutch Oostindische Companie and the East India Company. With the aid of the East India Company and its military might England stole highly-developed cotton-processing technology from the Indies and used it in its own production. The Company, with the Dutch hard on its heels, forced Indian drapers to sell their goods at higher prices, thus destroying the indigenous industry and gaining a monopoly in fine textiles.

The Company shipped finished goods – weapons, alcohol and trinkets such as glass beads – to Africa to sell, and bought slaves with a part of the profit. It transported the slaves to the Caribbean and to North and South America, sold them (on average, half of them died on the journey) at further profit to the colonialist class of plantation and mine owners, loaded its ships with precious metals and raw materials such as cotton, sugar and tobacco, brought them home and sold them at yet more profit to industrial capitalists and consumers with money to spend.

E. Williams has described the grisly details of this carefully thought-out machinery of human exploitation for the enrichment of Europeans and their viceroys in the colonies.[59] About twenty million Africans were enslaved, and up to fifty million perished in the slave-hunt and transportation. We often talk arrogantly about African tribal wars, but we forget that these only took on their murderous character because of the incentive of slave money for defeated "prisoners of war".

Africa was steadily underdeveloped.[60] But the economy of America and the Caribbean was distorted, their riches plundered by the setting up of monocultures for European consumption.

In Europe itself, prosperous groups among the merchants, the state bureaucracy, the free trades and the church profited in many ways from the increase of capital, which now enabled added value to be skimmed off in several ways:[61]

• Instead of the original trade by exchange according to the model "Goods (G) - Money as means of exchange (M) - other Goods (G^1)", it was now "Money (M) - Goods (G) - more Money (M^1)" (increasing money as *trading capital*).

• Through the loan of money with interest, money (M) became more money (M^1) (increasing money as *finance capital*).

• The intermediate stage of production gave rise to the formula "Money (M) - trade in raw materials (G) - production involving the exploitation of workers (P) - sale of finished Goods (G^1) - more Money (M^1)" (increasing money as *industrial capital*). This formula will concern us in more detail when we come to the later phase of industrial capitalism in the nineteenth century.

The period's main ideologues were Thomas Hobbes, for mercantilism's absolutist phase, and John Locke, for its constitutional phase. In his book *Leviathan*, Hobbes grounds the necessity of a strong state in a society which is in the process of becoming capitalist, in which man becomes a wolf to man, and in which money is the blood of Leviathan – the creature from the abyss.[62] More important for later development in the West is John Locke, who in his *Second Treatise of Government* lays the foundation for the anthropology and constitutional theory of Western capitalist societies. The American constitution of 1776, the constitutions of the French revolution, and others right up to the Bonn constitution, built on his thinking.[63] Several elements of his theory have particularly important consequences: property is what fundamentally defines human beings: the unlimited increase of property is based on the dynamic of money, which justifies the inequality between ownership and slavery; and law and the state exist to protect property.

Behind Locke's concept of property lies the idea in Roman law of "dominium". This is tantamount to absolute power and gives the owner the right to do with his property whatever he likes: *Dominium est ius utendi et abutendi re sua quaterus iuris ratio patitur* (Ownership is the right to use and *ab*use one's own property as long as this is consistent with the meaning of the law).[64]

Now, the relationship of property to the law may be thought to involve some restriction, e.g. in the sense of a social obligation. This is very far from Locke's thinking. It is concerned only with the observance of the law of contract, which is guaranteed by the state, whose sole function is again the protection of property.[65] Moreover, Locke states with express approval that with the introduction of money people accumulated more property than they could deal with and more than they needed to satisfy their basic needs.[66]

Not only that. As Binswanger has demonstrated, Locke sees that money is the driving force of the capitalist economy in that, as a production factor devoted to the increase of wealth (alongside its function as a means of exchange), by means of interest and prices it creates an "artificial" money value.[67] With his theories and practical proposals John Law then applied these ideas to paper money as well.[68] Binswanger has shown, using the story of Goethe's *Faust*, part II, that this cheque drawn against the future and guaranteed by the state can be covered only if the whole earth is constantly converted into saleable commodities – the most profound reason for capitalist society's persistent destruction of nature.[69] Binswanger interprets this as alchemy – changing base elements into gold – continued by other means, just as Mephistopheles proposes in Goethe's *Faust*.

Thus the heart of the *theological* question for the mercantile period is revealed. If in the Spanish phase it was God or gold, now it is God or money (not as a means of exchange but for maximizing the world's cash value, irrespective of the consequences for humanity and nature). As opposed to the Spanish period, however, when Las Casas and others fought on behalf of the minority, I have found no-one among the theologians of the mercantile period who might have understood and taken up this issue. On the contrary, at the end of that period the first Protestant missionary societies were established quite naively on the analogy of the trading companies, as William Carey, their initiator, shows.[70] By 1589 Richard Hakluyt had already described a conception of the relationship between Europe's trade and the evangelization of Asia, Africa and Latin America. Europe received the commodities and treasures of distant kingdoms, the other received the "incomparable treasure of the trueth of Christianity":

> For mine own part, I take it as a pledge of God's further favour unto us and them: to them especially, unto whose doores I doubt not in time shalbe by us carried the incomparable treasure of trueth of Christianity, and of the Gospell, while we use and exercise common trade with their merchants.[71]

Yet there were powerful individual examples of resistance, for example the Jesuits in Paraguay, John Eliot in North America, and the self-liberation of the slaves under Toussaint Louverture. Galeano summarizes the Jesuits' work as follows:

> In Spanish America the missionary work of the Jesuits developed as a sign of progress. They came in order to purify, through the example of self-denial and asceticism, a Catholic Church which had given itself up to idleness and the unbridled enjoyment of the luxuries that the "Conquista" had put at the clergy's disposal. It was the missions in Paraguay that achieved the most; in little more than a century and a half (1603-1768) they proved the capacities and goals of their creator. With the language of music they drew in the Guarani Indians, who had sought shelter in the primeval forest and stayed there, without involving themselves in the "civilizing process" of the lords and landowners. A hundred and fifty thousand Guarani Indians were able to return to their original way of community life and bring back to life their own ways in the areas of crafts and art. In the missions Latifundium was eliminated; the earth was worked partly to satisfy individual needs, partly to enable work in the collective interest and for the acquisition of tools – which were owned collectively. The life of the Indians was organized with wisdom and foresight; in the workshops and schools Indians were trained as musicians, craftsmen, farmers, weavers, painters and builders. There was no money; entrance was forbidden to traders, and they had to do their business from lodgings some distance away. The crown finally gave way to pressure from the financiers, and the Jesuits were driven out of America. The landowners and slave traders began a wild hunt for Indians. In the missions corpses hung from the trees; whole villages were sold in the Brazilian slave markets. Many Indians again found refuge in the forest. The Jesuits' libraries were used as fuel for stoves or to generate patrons.[72]

The film *The Mission* gives a real feeling of this community life as a sign of the kingdom of God and the destruction of this sign in the interest of Europe's economy and power.

John Eliot (1604-90) offers yet another contrast to the colonialist missionary approach.[73] He experienced a conversion under the influence of the non-conformist preacher Thomas Hooker, left the state church, and in 1631 emigrated to New England. He became a Congregationalist minister and teacher out of "compassion" for the Indians, translated the Bible and catechism into their language, and promoted the setting-up of independent Indian communities (Praying Indians), which he – like the Jesuits in Paraguay – protected from the settlers. The characteristics of this kind of Puritan community are the grounding in the Bible (the new community in Christ knows "neither Jew nor Greek", Gal. 3:26); the social expression of faith; the organization of Indian communities, according to their own politico-economic culture, under their own leadership, before they became Christian communities.

In England the Society for the Propagation of the Gospel in New England, which later took the name of the New England Company, was founded to support the Indian mission. Neither Eliot nor the Company could prevent these communities from being destroyed in 1675-76, but their model lived on. The Herrnhuts followed it in the eighteenth century when they opened their missions in the Caribbean – with all the amibiguity of the slavery-based plantation economy that existed there.

In this kind of plantation economy the most striking example of resistance and alternative thinking took place: the first successful and only self-liberation of slaves in world history, which resulted in an independent republic of slaves under Toussaint Louverture in French Saint-Domingue, present-day Haiti, between 1791 and 1798.[74] The slave Toussaint Louverture lived in the same area where Columbus established the first settlements and where Las Casas developed alternative communities (called Reductions) with the Indios. He was allowed to use his priest's library, and there he acquired knowledge not just of the biblical message of liberation and the tradition of Las Casas but also of military strategy. When news of the French Revolution and its principles of "liberté, égalité, fraternité" reached the open ears of the slaves, they began their guerrilla tactics and under Toussaint's leadership defeated the English and French invaders. Napoleon, who was unwilling to abandon the rich sugar island for economic and strategic reasons, tricked Toussaint and took him prisoner, and brought him in chains to France where he perished in misery. The English poet William Wordsworth dedicated this poem to him in 1803:[75]

> Toussaint, the most unhappy man of men!
> Whether the whistling rustic tend his plough
> Within thy hearing, or thy head be now
> Pillowed in some deep dungeon's earless den; –
> O miserable Chieftain! where and when
> Wilt thou find patience! Yet die not; do thou
> Wear rather in thy bonds a cheerful brow:
> Though fallen thyself, never to rise again,
> Live and take comfort. Thou hast left behind
> Powers that will work for thee; air, earth and skies;
> There's not a breathing of the common wind
> That will forget thee; thou hast great allies;
> Thy friends are exultations, agonies,
> And love, and man's unconquerable mind.

The prophecy came true. Toussaint's army of freed slaves conquered Napoleon's soldiers. The European powers and the colonies tried to isolate Haiti – a comparable situation to that of Cuba in the second half of the twentieth century – and the Vatican refused to set up an independent diocese. In spite of this the people of Haiti hung on (even though they could not overcome the cancerous effect of the dependence on exports the French had built into their economy), until in our century the USA established the Duvalier dictatorship. But the tradition of Las Casas and Toussaint emerged again in 1991 when the grassroots communities and popular movements succeeded on their own (without help from abroad or a political party) in electing the priest of the poor, Aristide, as president with over sixty percent of the vote. (As the US had just been engaged, ostensibly, in punishing – with 150,000 war dead – a dictator for attacking a small neighbouring country, it was in no position to annul by the usual direct or indirect methods the result of a halfway-free election in Haiti, even though its old ally, the military, promptly tried to stage a coup). It was left to the Vatican to revoke Aristide's standing as a priest!

3. The Free Trade of Industrial Capitalism under England's Leadership in the Nineteenth Century

The triangular trade made an enormous contribution to Britain's industrial development. The profits from this trade fertilized the entire productive system of the country.[76]

Thesis 4

With the aid of capital accumulated through the colonial and slave trade, England finances the Industrial Revolution. Free trade and work for wages in the form of "Manchester Capitalism" prove to be more profitable than mercantile protectionism and slavery. Despite England's undisputed leading role in the world economy after her victory over Napoleon in 1815, there is a kind of balance of power within Europe, which gives Europe one hundred years of peace. Wars are restricted to Asia, Africa and Latin America, and they are waged in order to force non-subject countries like Paraguay into the "free market". The rise of Germany, after the foundation of the Reich, to colonial great-power status and the new situation of competition this creates lead to the first world war and marks the end of this period. Its great theorist is Adam Smith, but with Karl Marx comes the first serious questioning of the capitalist world system. The labour movement emerges as a model of resistance in Europe itself, but within churches, missions and theology only evanescent minorities grasp the structural problems industrial capitalism poses for humanity and nature.

Just as James Watt's invention and development of the steam engine was financed directly by profits from the mercantile Triangular Trade, so also some of the capital for the new heavy industry came from the same source.[77] There were other factors also; in particular the peasants' loss of land through Enclosures, which drove them to work for wages; the new methods in agricultural production used in capitalized large-scale land ownership; the invention of the mechanical loom, which made England's textile industry superior to all others; and the development of coal-mining – to name just a few. Through the industrial capitalist revolution England was more successful than all its competitors.[78] How should this process be understood?

According to Polanyi[79] the heart of the revolution was the linking of *machine* and *market economy* – which evidently led people to believe that all human problems could be solved by material goods. He shows that "once elaborate machines and plants were used for production in a commercial society, the idea of a self-regulating market system was bound to take shape". For since the businessman is the central figure in this system, all factors in the entire mechanism have to be able to be bought and sold – at a profit. Clearly, it is no longer a matter, as mentioned above, of buying and selling finished goods (M-G-M^1). Rather, production is slotted in between: money (M) buys what are described as production factors (labour, raw materials, perhaps more money as credit, machines and plant) as goods (G), delivers them to the production process (P), and sells the produced goods (G^1) for more money (M^1).[80]

Thus all economic transactions are converted into money – with the object of making more money. Binswanger has demonstrated with the aid of Goethe's *Faust*, part II, how old concepts of magic are at work here: from some less valuable material gold is made. "It is a matter of maximizing the money value of 'the world'."[81] What are the assumptions of this kind of market economy and its consequences for industrial capitalism?

• People operate in order to make maximum profit.
• The market regulates supply and demand by price.
• Money in the hands of its owner is buying power.
• Production is determined by prices, since profits depend upon them.
• Distribution is determined by prices, for prices shape the income that regulates the distribution of goods.

But this has important consequences:
• In the *production process* work, land and money are in effect reduced to commodities.
• All that remains of working people and their social relationships is labour.
• All that remains of nature is raw materials for exploitation.
• Money is no longer a means of exchange, but an instrument for making more money.

Distribution is necessarily unequal, as Adam Smith frankly admits, because the negotiating power of those involved varies, and also because working people, having accepted a wage for their labour, have given up all claim on their product, which the entrepreneur uses to maximize his income.[82] Thus through the market:

• goods   obtain   prices   for the entrepreneur
• work   obtains   wages   for the worker
• land   obtains   rent   for the landowner
• money   obtains   interest   for the owner of capital

In the area of *consumption* a new motivation appears: production is no longer for the maintenance of life (basic needs) but for what those with buying power want to consume (for basic needs only to the extent there is buying power).

Polanyi states in summary:

> To allow the market mechanism to be sole director of the fate of human beings and their natural environment, indeed, even of the amount and use of purchasing power, would result in the demolition of society. For the alleged commodity "labour power" cannot be shoved around, used indiscriminately, or even left unused, without affecting the human individual who happens to be the bearer of this peculiar commodity. In disposing of a man's labour power the system would, incidentally, dispose of the physical, psychological and moral entity "man" attached to that tag. Robbed of the protective covering of cultural institutions, human beings would perish from the effects of social exposure; they would die as the victims of acute social dislocation through vice, perversion, crime and starvation. Nature would be reduced to its elements, neighbourhoods and landscapes defiled, rivers polluted, military safety jeopardized, the power to produce food and raw materials destroyed. Finally, the market administration of purchasing power would periodically liquidate business enterprise, for shortages and surfeits of money would prove as disastrous to business as floods and drought in primitive society. Undoubtedly, labour, land and money markets *are* essential to a market economy. But no society could stand the effects of such a system of crude fictions even for the shortest time unless its human and natural substance as well as its business organization was protected against the ravages of this satanic mill.[83]

Binswanger says of the modern "alchemic" process in which all things are converted into money values that "by this objectification the world is dematerialized and its life is taken".[84] He shows, again by using Goethe's *Faust*, how it ends. Faust is blinded by his anxiety to have the future in his grasp. He hears the sound of digging, and thinks it is for the great dam-building project, to create wealth – but it is his grave that is being dug. Thus F. Hinkelammert speaks of the capitalist metaphysic as death's ideological weapon.[85]

It is well known that in the period of early industrial or "Manchester" capitalism, the social and in part physical existence of working people and their families in Europe, and particularly in Britain, was radically diminished. What is less well-known is the effect this had in the colonies, which were – to their disadvantage – drawn even more deeply into the British-ruled international division of labour than during the mercantile period. Galeano[86] describes these effects in Latin America, where in the nineteenth century Britain controlled ninety percent of the trade. Countries that would not bow down to what it dictated in terms of expensive finished goods and cheap raw materials and labour were driven into this "free market" by force of arms.

The best-known example is Paraguay. While with great diplomatic skill British high finance achieved a balance of power in Europe that led to a hundred years of peace,[87] at the same time (1865-70) Britain financed a murderous war by the "triple federation" of Argentina, Brazil and Uruguay against Paraguay which had a flourishing independent economy. The result:

> It was not just the population that disappeared from conquered Paraguay. The customs tariffs, the blast furnaces of the iron foundries, the river barriers for free trade, economic independence and great tracts of its territory disappeared with them. The war was hardly over when the first foreign loan in its history descended on the still smoking ruins of Paraguay. It was British, obviously. Nominally it amounted to £1 million sterling, but much less than half of it reached Paraguay; in the years that followed the debt rose through refinancing to £3 million. After the defeat Paraguay too guaranteed freedom of trade. The cotton plantations were given up and Manchester annihilated the textile industry; the indigenous industry has never recovered.[88]

But since the three countries which made war inevitably became indebted to Britain, afterwards they also suffered financial collapse, so that they became even more dependent upon the world power that was operating in the background.

Was there that protection from the market, guided by an unseen hand, which according to Adam Smith should lead to prosperity for all? In terms of the world market, two countries succeeded in withdrawing from the dictatorship of British free trade: Germany and the USA, which, following the teaching of Friedrich List, strengthened their own economies by protectionist customs duties, building up their own industry and strong domestic markets, and developing their own colonial policies.[89]

In Europe the emerging labour movement was based on social democratic and socialist ideas.[90] To prevent it from taking over political power, states responded with social legislation and policies for regulating the economy.[91]

What about the churches, the missions and theology? In the nineteenth century two major areas of focus developed, which can only be dealt with superficially here: mission and colonialism (imperialism), and the church and social questions (the labour movement). The question of church and state, "throne and altar", also belongs here indirectly, to the extent that the state is involved in questions of (world) economy.

With regard to *social questions*, and particularly the situation of working people and their families in industrial capitalism, generally the churches either failed to recognize the issue or expressed their views only in the form of a polemic against the socialist or social democratic labour movement, which led to the well-known alienation between the church and the working class. We shall confine ourselves to Germany. Tolerated at best on the Protestant side was the organization of a movement of Christian love in the form of free associations for home mission, along the style of its founder, Johann Hinrich Wichern (1808-81).[92] Wichern was politically conservative – he went so far as to reject the 1848 revolution as "wicked" – and his paternalistic pastoral approach did not criticize structures. Even so, the emergence of a "social-Christian" as anti-social democratic, anti-liberal and even anti-semitic as Adolf Stoecker (1839-87) made the Protestant Oberkirchenrat in Berlin forbid the clergy to engage in any kind of political activity.[93] The foundation of the Protestant Social Congress led in 1895 to another such decree. In it had gathered those with liberal social views, who above all preached a liberal imperial nation-state and wished to restrict faith to inner life and personal convictions leaving the areas of economic life and the state for those with power to rule by themselves.[94] Its best-known representative was Friedrich Naumann (1860-1919). One lonely figure, firmly rooted in Jesus' message of the kingdom of God, who also concerned himself with the structural problems of capitalist society and became involved in the workers' struggle, was Christoph Blumhardt (1842-1919).[95] Isolated from his church in Württemberg, he influenced the religious social movement – which, admittedly, was unable in turn to influence greatly either the churches or the working class.[96]

In the Catholic church things were somewhat different.[97] As early as 1808-9 Adam Müller began a key debate with Adam Smith, and in 1864 a bishop, Ketteler, was already working on the theme of "The Workers' Question and Christianity" and propagating the idea of the common use of property. Although the first papal social encyclical, Leo XIII's *Rerum Novarum* (1891), was sharply anti-socialist, it supported the labour movement's aspirations and introduced an official Catholic social teaching which for a long time had no counterpart in the Protestant church.

When we look at the area of *mission and colonialism*, the picture is similar.[98] In Germany the most extreme view was expressed by Friedrich Fabri, above all in his book "Does Germany Need the Colonies?"[99] He commends the "usefulness" of missions "for the advancement of the trading companies or for colonial annexations" (p.95), and endorses the process, which Bismark had only hesitantly begun, of making Germany a colonial power with German settlements overseas. He develops his views against a background of patriotic, pietistic historical philosophy and comes to the conclusion that the focus of world history will continue to be in the countries where the *Imperium Romanum* existed. In other words, the countries of Europe would "remain the agents of the world's history and fate" until the Last Day.[100] Although he was until 1884 Inspektor of the Rhenish Mission, Fabri had more influence in political and business circles than in the Mission itself. Here there were also warning voices, above all that of Gustav Warneck.[101] But in the nineteenth century there were no real alternatives or counter-models as in previous centuries in the work of Las Casas, the Jesuits, Eliot or particularly Toussaint Louverture, and certainly not at the height of Germany's imperialist phase about the time of the 1884 Congo conference in Berlin.

Panikkar summarizes the weaknesses of Western mission history in four points: (1) the assumption of moral superiority; (2) the linking of mission with aggressive claims to domination; (3) the belief that not only Christianity but also European-ness was better, which led to the belief in the superiority of the "white race"; (4) the denominational fragmentation of Western Christianity.[102]

And so we come to the ecumenical movement of the twentieth century. There were no new significant trends during the years that preceded it.

4. Fordism, Keynesianism and Neo-Liberalism in twentieth-Century America

4.1 SOCIAL PROSPERITY AT THE CENTRE – DEVELOPMENT OF MORE UNDERDEVELOPMENT AT THE PERIPHERY, FROM 1945 TO THE 1970s

Thesis 5

The increasing competition between the centres of capitalism in Europe explodes into the first world war. The USA emerges as the strongest power, but does not immediately take over leadership of the international financial system. The instability and the continuing unregulated competition between the different centres of capitalism lead to the world economic crisis of 1929. After the second world war, begun by fascism, the USA – now even stronger – takes over leadership of the international financial system (the dollar, linked to the gold standard, becomes the world currency, the International Monetary Fund (IMF) guarantees exchange rates and accords credits in liquidity crises when trade balances go wrong), the General Agreement on Tariffs and Trade (GATT) lays down the terms of "free" world trade (very much to the disadvantage of countries of the two-thirds world which are in the process of decolonization), the arms race with the Soviet Union begins, but there is war only against two-thirds world countries which lean towards socialism (Vietnam) or want to withdraw from the Western powers' neo-colonialism. Fordism rules production in the urban centres with higher wages which create mass buying-power and mass consumption, and the Keynesian state helps with employment and social-welfare policies.

The improved situation in countries at the centre is clearly the result of the struggles of the labour movement: some of its ideals are integrated into the capitalist system and it more or less gives up international solidarity. Many liberation movements in the former colonies achieve political but not economic independence – though there are exceptions, like China. In the ecumenical movement there is growing criticism of capitalism.

"A 'new capitalism', which many people called by the name of 'imperialism', developed at the beginning of the twentieth century. It included many factors, among which the following were prominent: concentration of capital, cartels, trusts, and monopolies; interpenetration of industrial capital and banking capital within the new reality of finance capital; the renewed role of the state, through social legislation, its major role in large public work projects, territorial expansion, and militarism; export of capital, colonization, and the dividing up of the world" – thus M. Beaud in *A History of Capitalism* sums up the state of colonialist capitalism or, better, of the various national-imperialist capitalisms (above all Britain, Germany, France and the USA) at the beginning of our century.[103] This form of capitalism's model of accumulation and regulation gave rise to a series of contradictions which Beaud systematizes as follows:[104]

a) At the level of production, the classical contradiction between the capital-owning bourgeoisie and the exploited wage-workers is softened by national states, which through social legislation seek to prevent the labour movement overcoming the capitalist system through revolution.

b) At the level of the realization of added value, i.e. when goods are sold, there is ever sharper competition not just between national capitalists but also between national and foreign capitalists – on the home market as well as the world market.

c) At the level of the profit-making reinvestment of accumulated capital in particular, national and international competition becomes sharper, the more so because of increasing re-armament in the leading capitalist nation-states.

This is the (world) economic background against which the first world war began.[105] "Capitalism brings war, as the rain cloud brings the storm," it was said.[106] And the war brought eight million dead and heavy debts for the European states involved – yet US gold reserves quadrupled and in 1921 amounted to forty percent of the entire world reserves.[107] The USA began to emerge as the centre of capitalist world economy.

But the European capitalist nations still sought to regain their strength, which led to sharper competition between them on the world market, and resulting distress for the working people and even more for those forced into unemployment. Indeed, after the collapse of the international financial system, which depended on gold and the British currency, there was no ordered form of international payments. This and other factors led to the great Depression, the world economic crisis which began in 1929 and led to the second world war – unleashed by fascism, a kind of extreme national capitalism.

In this phase the USA took over leadership in the capitalist world economy at all levels. On the basis of accumulating capital by making profits from waged work financed by private capital (law of value), it introduced the new accumulation model of *Fordism*. It took over *Keynesianism* as a model of state regulation. It developed the *Bretton Woods system* (the IMF and the World Bank) as a system of international finance and the GATT as a system of international trade. It built a worldwide network of military bases and alliances – legitimized by its opposition to the Soviet Union, the second super-power, but in fact to counteract the efforts by the peoples of the so-called third world to achieve social advance and independence. This system functioned – with the active participation of the West European capitalist states and Japan – until the 1970s. Since then we have been in a process of change. Let us go through the individual elements of the "pax Americana".

Fordism means the following model of production and accumulation:[108] rationalization of the production process (the production line); relatively high wages for the sector of the work-force that accepts these and other disciplines, with the intention of dividing the working class and deterring it from making further political demands; higher production. The mass buying-power this achieves yields higher profits as added value is taken off on the product market and binds part of the working class to the middle class through mass consumption.

After President Roosevelt's *New Deal* in 1932, which ended the world economic crisis, capitalism developed instruments for getting a grip on the reasons for such crises. Alongside measures for banks, industry, trade and infrastructure, there was a historic compromise between the owners of capital and (the compliant) part of the working class – later named after the English economist Keynes: the state would intervene not only with social legislation for the protection and safety of workers in the production process, but also – and above all in times of recession – with employment policies to prevent unemployment through public investment and to strengthen the market. Low interest policies serve the same purpose. Many of these and other elements were introduced into the so-called "social" market economy of the Federal Republic of Germany – particularly at the time of the social-liberal coalition.

No such concessions were made by the USA and the other Western powers when the international finance system was reformed at the *Bretton Woods* conference in 1944. Here too Keynes submitted a plan. He had recognized "that international payments can only flow smoothly if deficits and surpluses do not become permanent". He proposed that "if cash surpluses have not been spent on the purchase of goods and services from abroad within a certain time, they should be cancelled. Thus there would be direct pressure to reduce currency surpluses by means of increased imports."[109] A glance at the problem of the debt crisis in the 1980s (which will be considered later) immediately shows the relevance of this proposal. Instead of putting the burden of an imbalance of trade and payments between strong creditor counties and weaker debtor countries wholly upon the weak, as had been the case, in Keynes' plan the strong would also have had to undergo "structural adjustments". If they did not import goods from the weaker countries, their surplus would be taken away by tax. But this went against the interests of the country which had the greatest surplus, the USA; so its so-called White Plan was accepted.

The heart of the Bretton Woods system[110] was the *International Monetary Fund* (IMF). Its purpose was to control the maintenance of agreed and fixed exchange rates which gave the dollar the function of world currency, on the basis of a guarantee by the US government to maintain its conversion against gold (US$53 = 1 ounce of gold). The Fund had an agreed basis of credit ready in case of temporary balance-of-payments problems. To understand the IMF, it is important to appreciate that it is not a democratic organization of all the countries which later became members of the UN. Rather, it is organized like a joint stock company, with voting power dependent on deposits ("one dollar–one vote"). Now 148 countries belong to it, but the "Club of Ten" leading industrial countries (USA, Germany, Britain, France, Italy, Japan, Canada, Holland, Belgium and Sweden) hold 54 percent of the shares (as on 31 December 1982), and with over twenty percent the USA has a practical right of veto. In its early period the IMF served above all to even out balances of trade among the industrialized countries. In 1945 the World Bank was founded, mainly to grant loans for development projects within the IMF framework.

In 1948 the *General Agreement on Tariffs and Trade* (GATT) was negotiated to strengthen free trade. Through it, the participant countries accepted an obligation to advantage each other through customs duties (non-discrimination). While in principle there was to be no restriction on their size, exceptions are possible which in effect cancel this. In practice the GATT has a very negative effect on the so-called developing countries; they are unable to put tariffs on finished goods from the industrialized countries in order to protect their own industry. On the other hand, the USA and the European Community allow exceptions at precisely those points where the developing countries are strong – agricultural products above all. Thus the old trick of the capitalist "free" world market continues: freedom for the strong, protectionism against the weak.

After the developing countries came together in the Group of 77, through the UN economic organization, UNCTAD, they were able to defeat the 1968 preference rules. But in the change-over period that followed (see below) the industrialized countries progressively weakened the democratically-organized UN, so that UNCTAD became less and less significant and the GATT arrangements, which they controlled, stronger and stronger.

With regard to US steps to secure its empire militarily, the Vietnam war immediately comes to mind. But at least as important as direct interventions were the dictatorial or military regimes the CIA installed in countries which, having won their freedom from direct colonialism, were in danger of escaping the control of the Western capitalist system and which wanted to introduce more social – though by no means always more socialist – forms of society. We need only remember the murder of Lumumba and the installation of Mobutu in Zaire, the murder of Mossadegh and the installation of the Shah in Iran, and the murder of Allende and the installation of Pinochet in Chile.[111]

The US leadership was clear from the beginning that it could defend its wealth only by a tough power policy. State Department Planning Study 23 of 24 February 1948 (composed by George Kennan) says:

> ... we have about 50% of the world's wealth, but only 6.3% of its population... In this situation, we cannot fail to be the object of envy and resentment. Our real task in the coming period is to devise a pattern of relationships which will permit us to maintain this position of disparity without detriment to our national security. To do this, we will have to dispense with all sentimentality and day-dreaming; and our attention will have to be concentrated everywhere on our immediate national objectives. We need not deceive ourselves that we can afford today the luxury of altruism and world-benefaction... We should cease to talk about vague and – for the Far East – unreal objectives such as human rights, the raising of living standards, and democratization. The day is not far off when we are going to have to deal in straight power concepts. The less we are then hampered by idealistic slogans, the better.[112]

In the West the *ideological* slogans of this period were "unlimited growth" and "progress" on the one hand and "anti-communism" on the other. For the countries at the centre of Western capitalism it indeed meant a huge increase in growth and prosperity and, with part of the accumulated capital, the extension of the social state. The countries of Asia, Africa and Latin America which had thrown off colonialism were consoled with the "trickle-down" theory of modern development, that by the enrichment of the rich the poor can be helped to follow the same development path as the industrialized countries. Hence the expression, based on the Western model, "developing countries".

There was in the centre-countries themselves hardly any *resistance* to this Western system under US hegemony. Since the labour movement had won from capitalism the concessions of Fordism and Keynesianism, it confined itself – in the form of the trade union movement – to negotiating its share of the growth cake. And social democracy gave up all reflection on the question of the class struggle and made itself into a "popular party" fit for government in Keynesian capitalism.

But there was resistance in many forms in the countries of the periphery – occasionally even successful resistance. The success of the Group of 77 in terms of the institutional world system has already been mentioned. I am also thinking – to name just a few examples of the many struggles – of the People's Republic of China. In spite of its justly criticized human rights record, it succeeded after appalling colonialist exploitation and oppression in making itself truly independent and in providing, through amongst other things a model health system, for the basic needs of a fifth of its people. Cuba too should be named. To this day it is defending itself against economic blockade and invasions from the US – in all its imposed and self-induced weakness.

At this point we should consider as well – despite Western propaganda – the aid that the Soviet Union provided for not just countries like Cuba but also for independent liberation movements like the African National Congress. This was certainly not out of pure altruism, but it shamed the West, which has to this day not supported independence but destroyed it wherever it could. Resistance was oriented ideologically upon the analytical idea of dependence rather than modernization, and upon the strategic idea of liberation for independence rather than development.[113]

The position of the *churches* in this phase cannot be reduced even approximately to one or two factors. In our context, however, by far the most significant thing is undoubtedly the rise of the ecumenical movement, in precisely the period of time in question. Unfortunately, no comprehensive history of its development in the context of the political economy of this century exists.[114] The World Mission Conference in Edinburgh in 1910 – the birthplace of today's ecumenical movement – raises questions about colonialism in the light of experience in Asia and Africa. The 1925 Life and Work conference in Stockholm and the 1928 World Mission Conference in Jerusalem in particular criticize resolutely the injustice of the capitalist system and call for its rejection. At the Oxford conference in 1937 further questions are raised, and pure capitalism is rejected in the same way as communism. But there are already signs that, under the influence of British and North American theologians (above all Reinhold Niebuhr and William Temple), a kind of "realism" in the sense of commitment to a Keynes-type capitalist social state is taking over. That applies particularly to the idea of the "responsible society", which may be seen as the normative concept of ecumenical social ethics from the inaugural assembly of the World Council of Churches (WCC) in 1948 until 1966. Only minorities like the Christian Socialists maintain a fundamental questioning of capitalism. If one were to investigate the Catholic church and Catholic social teaching on its position on economic justice, the picture would be similar. Here too new tendencies emerge only in the 1960s, under the influence of the Second Vatican Council.

4.2 THE VICTORY OF NEW-LIBERALISM AND MONETARISM, THE INCREASING DIVISION BETWEEN SOCIETIES IN THE NORTH AND SOUTH – AND NOW IN THE EAST AS WELL

Thesis 6

After the Vietnam war the post-war system goes into crisis. The economic dominance of the USA comes to an end and the dollar's parity with gold is abandoned. Capital brings down Keynesianism and Fordism through transnationalization, causes the debt crisis by introducing monetarism, etc., and widens the gap between the rich and the poor, both between and within countries, with the aid of a new accumulation model and a neo-liberal ideology. Its political essentials are articulated at the world economic summit of seven big industrial nations (G7). Low Intensity Conflict (LIC) and Mid Intensity Conflict (MIC) as used most recently against Iraq become established as the means to hold back efforts to achieve economic independence in the two-thirds world. Because of the collapse of the challenge of "real socialism" (state capitalism) there is now a single, total, capitalist world system – not, to be sure, under the leadership of one super-power but under three (competing) central regions: North America under the leadership of the USA, Western Europe under the leadership of the reunited Germany, and North-East Asia under the leadership of Japan.

Naturally, it is not possible to have as clear an overview of the new mutation of capitalism in a development that is still in process as in a phase which has ended. It is easiest on the monetary side through the concept of monetarism. But the names already given to the new model of accumulation by the production process are clearly still tentative: e.g. "Post-Fordism", "toyotism", "global sourcing", "hyper-industrialization". There is also still no name for the model of state regulation in this phase. For the catch-word *deregulation* relates only to the state's social and fiscal functions over against the economy, while in a host of ways it intervenes *for* capital. It is again easy to find terms for the ideological aspect; the pertinent expression here is *neo-liberalism*. Let us try to get a general idea of its individual elements.

We shall turn first to the dismantling of Fordism and the Keynesian welfare state. Joachim Hirsch writes: "The decisive factor in economic terms was that the forced unification of the world market and the internationalization of capital took away the ground from under an economic and social policy based on national parameters."[115] The new unification of the world market has also been described as "a new international division of labour"[116] with the transnational corporations (TNCs) as the main actors. We shall return to the transnationalization of capital in the context of monetarism and the debt crisis.

Hirsch gives as a second element a new accumulation model "which, built on a series of new technologies like information, communications and biotechnology and genetic engineering, brings about radical change in work organization, class structures, consumption norms and company forms".[117] This involves above all flexible working practices and thus the dismantling of firm wage structures and the multinationalization of labour, the spread of unprotected and peripheral work, the off-loading of risks on to suppliers ("just in time" production), the separation of part of the work-force into structural unemployment, and through all this the awakening of the trade unions.[118]

That new strategies for the accumulation of capital lie behind the increasing, technology-led disadvantagement of most of the work-force while its highly-qualified part gets higher incomes becomes clear from the following consideration of developments in the 1980s. If one takes the GDP growth rate as a more or less straight rising line, wages fell persistently below it while incomes from capital assets rose persistently above it – exponentially even in the case of income from interest (to this we shall return). To express this in figures, the difference between the growth of incomes from wages and from the ownership of assets in West Germany in the 1980s was a ratio of 1:3 (cf. the *Frankfurter Rundschau* of 17 November 1989 – and these are only the official figures). The same difference may be observed amongst wage-earners and owners of capital. According to a study based on official figures by the Center on Budget and Policy Priorities in Washington, the picture for the 1980s is as follows:[119]

> While the US's high earners (1% of the population) were able to more than double their annual income ($451,000) between 1977 and 1988, the poorest 20% had to put up with an income reduction of 10% ($14,000)... Divided into 20 percentiles, the study shows not only a 10% income decline for the lowest fifth of the population but also stagnating incomes for the middle class. The second fifth of the population had to accept income reductions of 3%, whilst the third fifth were able to register an income growth of 4%. The fourth and top fifths on the income scale earned 9% and 34% more. All these figures are adjusted for inflation and after tax. The report gives as causes for this development higher profits on capital, lower taxes for high earners and stagnating welfare payments.

The capital side bases this whole new trend on increasing competition in the world market. And competition has indeed become sharper. (A virtual economic war is raging between Japan and the US, and the Single European Market has resulted exclusively from the EC's idea of asserting itself against Japan and the USA, if not of moving into first place.) On the other hand even bigger monopolies enter into "strategic alliances". Hirsch says: "Vital sectors of capital are globalized, and corporations operating on the world market enter into diverging links within the now multipolar structure of metropolitan capital."[120] To put it simply: between the very big there is a renewed push towards further monopolization.

What results from all of this? "The tendency for national state systems for accumulation and regulation to disintegrate steps up the political and social conflict at both national and international levels, undermines the regulative capacity of inherited political and social institutions, and leads to a growth of openly violent ways of exercising power and forms of social division."[121] In short, there arises a new kind of struggle by everyone against everyone.

The *neo-liberal* ideology that stands behind this, first known as Reaganomics or Thatcherism, claims to take its stand on deregulation, i.e. on de-bureaucratizing the market from state intervention. That applies, however, only to state intervention in matters of social welfare. The post-Fordist state increases its interventions *for* capital; to keep industry in the country it engages politically in technology and the infrastructure and benefits great monopolies, as may be studied in the policies towards Daimler Benz/MBB. Under the pretext of fighting terrorism the state also develops increasingly into a police state, striving with the aid of new information technology for total supervision of the people. The Single European Market tends to further strengthen all this, as the signs already show.

But the division of people into those who are getting (more or less) poorer and those who are getting (more or less) richer, into the controlled and the controllers, is growing not just in the countries of the centre, but even more so in the countries of the two-thirds world. There the *monetary* area, as well as that of production and general economics, is playing a decisive role, above all at the tip of the iceberg: the debt-ridden peripheral countries. We have only to think of the many things published in connection with the IMF/World Bank conference in Berlin. The essential points are:[122]

The central economic factor in the emergent debt crisis was, as in the field of national economics, a further, specific push in the transnationalization of capital through the development of so-called free banking zones.[123] In the 1960s European banks first began to deal on the international money market directly in US dollars, without going through their own currencies – hence the name Eurodollar or Euromarket. In this way the banks avoided not only state controls (e.g. in relation to minimum reserves) but also taxation (cf. for instance the withdrawal of capital from Germany, when the CDU and FDP, the parties of capital themselves, considered it necessary to limit tax fraud through taxation at source, but had to give ground precisely because of capital's ability to withdraw to the "free" international market). Above all finance capital was able to operate in these markets purely according to the principle of maximization of profit. In a situation of excess capital and low interest rates that led to debt for the countries of the two-thirds world, their élites, wishing to catch up in industrial development, procured large orders from TNCs in the industrialized countries in the hope of being able to pay off their loans through later production for the world market. Two things prevented this: the deterioration of the terms of trade, precisely because so many "developing countries" wanted to produce for the world market that the prices for their products fell. Above all, however, the change of money policy in the post-Keynesian phase had a devastating effect on the "developing countries". Because of pressure from the money markets the US Federal Reserve Bank introduced in 1979 a restrictive, monetarist money policy which resulted in rapidly rising interest rates – exacerbated by Reagan's arms policy and consequent US debt and a shortage of capital which drove interest rates higher.[124] The results are well known. The virtual bankruptcy of Mexico in 1982 made the debt crisis (actually the crisis of the capitalist system) obvious to everyone. Now, aided by the debts, the IMF, acting in its new role of financial police for Western capital under the political leadership of the seven leading industrial countries (G7) which meet each year at the economic summit, squeezes out of the debtor countries whatever it can get – or, to be more precise, out of the poor of these countries, for their rich have joined in the flight of capital and profitably deposited much of their countries' debts in the very German, Swiss, Japanese and US banks that are destroying their countries. The means of this destruction is well known: the so-called structural adjustment measures, whose poison must be taken for healing: wage blocks, reduced social expenditure, the abolition of food subsidies, devaluation (= exports instead of consumption), allowing profits to be drawn off and these countries' economies to be made to serve the industrialized countries' interests.[125] All plans so far (the Baker and Brady Plans) simply stop from dying, through the partial write-off and restructuring of debts, the chicken that lays the golden egg – and the bankers and Western governments are obviously of the opinion that some chickens that are not going to yield any more should die quietly. The perfidy which this almost absolute power of life and death over millions evinced in the international financial institutions' highest-paid functionaries has been impressively described by one of them who got out for reasons of conscience, Davison Budhoo, in his book *Enough is Enough*.[126] Very few people know or imagine that the same process of debt, extortion and impoverishment/enrichment has been going on for a long time in Eastern Europe and is now gathering pace in the Soviet Union.

However, monetarist policy had a dangerous result for the economy of the USA and potentially for the whole Western economy as well. If it is so easy to earn money through high interest rates, what point is there in investing productively? Through this undercurrent the speculative money economy made itself independent of the real economy. Indeed, with the help of dubious financial practices the fashion arose in the USA of buying up big companies on credit and then reselling them exploitatively at a profit, the so-called "leveraged buy-out on junk bonds".[127] Thus the yuppie culture became an expression of what has also been described as the "casino society". The stock market crashes of recent years were just one sign of this.[128]

In terms of *security strategy* the USA had learned from Vietnam the lesson that open wars of oppression against peoples striving for independence and social justice cannot be won. Thus its mechanisms of oppression and control were refined with the help of the Low Intensity Conflict strategy/LIC.[129] This means that the military is deployed only in the background and mostly with the help of proxies, so that death squads are organized and supported, the country concerned is politically isolated, its economy is destabilized, but above all the socially-minded governments, freedom movements or solidarity movements involved are discredited socially and psychologically through disinformation campaigns, etc. The USA's dealings with an independent, more socially just Nicaragua provide the best-known example; the current attempts to ruin the victory of liberation movements in Southern Africa provide another.

Through the Gulf war it came out that since 1988 this concept has been supplemented by the Mid-Intensity Conflict strategy/MIC.[130] Its object is to hold down rising "third-world" countries that develop with the aid of modern technology in such a way that they are able to threaten the industrialized countries' world monopoly – like Iraq with regard to the oil price. Whether Germany should in the future participate openly in this "intervention" for the maintenance of the world dominance of metropolitan capital is being decided at present. It should be decided in full awareness of this background, which is currently being so effectively obfuscated by propagandist expressions like "UN peace missions" and "new world order".[131]

This is in fact the old world order: the capitalist world system – yet with important modifications. After the collapse of the flawed attempt at an alternative it has become total, and thus it asserts its will even more brutally than ever before – though through three centres (North America, led by the USA; Western Europe, led by the reunited Germany; and East Asia, led by Japan), although Bush, after his demonstration of military power in the Gulf war, is trying to win back the USA's (economically no longer justified) leadership role. A new Pentagon paper[132] clearly reveals this move of the US government.

In this latest phase *resistance* has clearly become more difficult. For reasons I have given (the fragmentation of the workers and other disadvantaged or marginal groups – farmers, for example – into those who earn a lot and those who owe a lot, and the growing weakness of the means of national state regulation), the classical instruments of the labour movement and Keynesian social democracy no longer work. At the international level UNCTAD has been progressively weakened over against the international institutions controlled by the rich industrialized countries (IMF/GATT). We no longer hear demands for a new world economic order from coalitions of any kind in the two-thirds world. The end of the aid which the Socialist bloc gave to liberation movements – whatever its motives – also makes things more difficult.

The same period, on the other hand, is characterized by the rise and growth of new social movements all around the world. The deepening contradictions of the post-Fordist, neo-liberal capitalist system have clearly helped this. We shall investigate in detail the possibilities they offer in the concluding part.

The churches too have played a part in this development. They are, admittedly, deeply divided. On the one hand we must note a worldwide neo-conservative and neo-liberal wave, coming essentially from the USA. At the moment it is supported by an open, pseudo-theological justification of capitalism. Its best-known exponent is Washington's Institute for Religion and Democracy under Michael Novak. But more important, because it has more popular effect, is a worldwide charismatic movement of the New Right, which in particular floods the religious market with electronic media and offers even to the victims of the system a market-conforming kind of religiosity – opium in Karl Marx's sense. It must also not be overlooked that, despite occasional criticism of the capitalist system –

as again in Pope John Paul II's latest encyclical, *Centesimo Anno* – the Vatican contributes a great deal to the strengthening of today's more rabid model of accumulation by disciplining liberation theologians and by filling *all* vacant bishoprics with at best conservatives and at worst reactionaries. This, moreover, is understood very clearly by secret services of the West, as may be seen from the secret documents of the American military.[133] The major Protestant churches too are being pushed to the right by the mere existence of more fundamentalist and evangelical groups.

On the other hand there is an awakening of powerful forces for justice, peace and the integrity of creation in the ecumenical movement and in Roman Catholic churches throughout the world. Since the Geneva conference on Church and Society in 1966 and the declaration of Latin American bishops at Medellín in 1968, a broad-based movement has developed in support of the Bible's preferential option for the poor and for not just personal but also structural liberation. Growing in different ways in the 1970s, in the 1980s this movement has grouped together in the conciliar process for "Justice, Peace and the Integrity of Creation". For the 1990 world convocation in Seoul and the 1991 assembly of the World Council of Churches in Canberra are the only official voices that still dared to reject the present capitalist world economic system and demand something fundamentally new.[134] Yet one should not hide the fact that at present the criticism of capitalism is unwelcome even in the official circles of the WCC.[135] So critical discussion is for the most part only in general terms and concerned with symptoms. Nevertheless, in the Canberra Section II report we read:

> Through the six preceding assemblies, the World Council of Churches has called the attention of its member churches and the public at large to serious contradictions and imbalances prevailing in the world economic system. Established structures continue to prevent the economic growth and social justice of the poor and exploited peoples and nations. It is necessary to build a new international economic order.[136]

What possibilities for action there are in the formation of coalitions between ecumenical grassroots groups and parts of the churches on one side and the new social movements on the other is something that will concern us in detail later.

Now we shall attend to some of the objections that may be made to this analysis and interpretation. The main argument seems to be that the competing alternative system of bureaucratic socialism has not worked, so capitalism has been proved to be right. The logic of this argument does not hold water:

• Bureaucratic socialism was no real alternative but operated on the same economic assumptions: industrial growth, capital accumulation, consumerism. The only difference *economically* was that the state, not private owners, was promoting the growth mechanism. This is why another name for bureaucratic socialism is state capitalism. The difference was in the area of distribution, not in the basic parameters of production and consumption.

• It is a simple fact that both these economies of unlimited growth of output are not sustainable. The earth simply does not allow for the unlimited exploitation of nature through exponential growth mechanisms – quite apart from the deadly consequences of capitalism's unjust distribution of the surplus among different groups, domestically and internationally.

• The logic, therefore, should be as follows: the less sophisticated model of state capitalism has broken down and left us with an ecological and even social disaster. The more sophisticated and flexible model of private market capitalism will break down by destroying the natural basis of life on this planet – including its ecological and social dimensions.[137]

Among other objections are the following.

In the centre-countries there has been in this latest phase not just economic prosperity but also better incomes for working people. And at the international level do not the emerging countries, particularly the "four little tigers" (South Korea, Taiwan, Hong Kong and Singapore) show that the capitalist development model works when internal national factors make "development" possible? That allegedly proves that the *dependence theory*, which makes the conditions of the world market responsible for the under-development of the poor countries, is wrong.

The first objection really about the West was already answered in the analysis itself. There is economic prosperity, but in the latest phase the unequal growth typical of the capitalist accumulation model has been extreme: not only have severe social evils like structural unemployment arisen, the working class has also become even more fragmented by the prosperity of the part of it that has accommodated to the system.

The objection concerning the "tigers" in fact complicates the dependence theory, but in no way disproves it. On the one hand this argument largely overlooks the fact that geopolitical, globally determined factors have helped decisively to bring these and not other countries to the fore. The West, particularly the USA, has invested enormous sums in order to bring them up to be bastions against communism (against North Korea/USSR, the People's Republic of China and Vietnam). On the other hand the development of capitalism's latest phase shows clearly that through the transnationalization of capital the group of victims is becoming more and more divided, and a simple differentiation into centre, periphery and semi-periphery is no longer adequate. Certainly, the basic concept of production through waged work and the cheapest possible raw material is still current, as is marketing with the object of taking off added value. But this process, which always causes dependence and unequal development, has become more complex and is now dividing social groups right across all the earlier, more obvious dependence structures of colonialism and post-war neo-colonialism. So we must look on the one hand at the core of the law of value (profit making) and its crude, visible structures of dependence, and on the other hand at the specific, historical transmutations of capitalism.[138]

5. Capitalism in History and the Present

A revolutionary theory is one which, when expressed, confronts society with its mutability and reveals the existing structures of power (Hans-Jürgen Krahl).[139]

Thesis 7

A survey of five hundred years of history shows that there is no such thing as quintessential capitalism, nor is one by nature necessary. It is true that all its historical forms share certain fundamental production characteristics (the need to produce added value, the alienation of the producers from their products, the formation of classes with unequal shares of the added value they produce). But both methods of accumulation and systems of regulation (i.e. the social institutions and actors that go above and beyond the purely economic) change. They must be made part of the analysis if one wants to find action points to bring about change.

Capitalism has constantly tried to present itself as necessary by nature. Adam Smith wanted to be the Newton of political economy. Newton had understood mechanics in terms of laws lying behind nature itself. Max Weber spoke of the autonomous laws of areas of life, and theologians of adaptation have gladly followed him. But the criticism of capitalism can also assume this kind of pseudo-legality. Marx's historical materialism has often been understood non-dialectically – as if the conquest of capitalism would come almost by itself, if only its crises were severe enough.

Going through the history of the last five hundred years has proved both positions to be false. There is no such thing as quintessential capitalism. The enormous changes it has undergone show to what extent its form at any one time is shaped by what people concerned at the time accept or – with greater or lesser success – fight against. It is equally clear that all the crises that led to new forms of capitalism have not so far led to its self-destruction. The most recent crises have rather contributed to its self-importance – which, to be sure, can in the Bible's view also lead to the fall of the whore of Babylon (Rev.18). Yet to understand exactly what can and should be done in this situation we need a more precise definition of what arrangements the capitalist system makes at each stage.

A survey of the phases we have gone through shows that capitalism is not to be understood as a pure economic system. Even a cursory glance at the simplest categories of production, capital and labour shows that behind them stand two groups of people, owners of capital and workers, who in

Changing Shape of the Capitalist World System 39

different social situations may have quite different positions – workers, for example, may be slaves or highly-paid employees in a modern company. And both may find themselves in either a free trade zone or governed by the rules of a social state. Finally, cultural attitudes play a role: I might live in an ecological commune or submit completely to mass consumption, and so on.

Normal economics gives no help in understanding the situatedness of capitalist economies. On the contrary, it tries to isolate the human being as *homo oeconomicus* and thus reveals itself as ideology, not science, in that it does not admit the hypothetical and manipulative character of its statements. A school that makes its programme to see the economy in overall social and natural life terms is "Institutional Economics". Among the authors I have cited who belong to it are above all Polanyi, Heilbronner and Hirsch.[140] In his most recent book, *No Alternative to Capitalism?*,[141] Hirsch has made the most theoretically detailed and up-to-date attempt yet to analyze and explain capitalism in the full context of different kinds of society. He identifies three fundamental categories which interact to shape the historical form capitalism takes at any stage:

1) the capitalist method of production itself;
2) the means of accumulation;
3) the means of regulation.

> The *capitalist method of production* is a modus of *socialization*, determined essentially by the private production of goods, enabled by exchange, by the alienation of the producers from the means of production and by waged labour. This establishes the capitalist class structure and a social dynamic determined by the competitive pressure to produce added value, the maximizing of profit, and accumulation. This socializing process is the basis of "objective" social forms (value, money, capital) which both throw up individuals "behind one's back" and determine their actions.[142]

I would add with Binswanger that capitalism is defined in money terms not only by the use of alienated wage labour but also of nature. For only then can we understand not just the socially but also ecologically destructive consequences of capitalism. All areas of life and society are never actually drawn into the capitalized production of added values, but there is in the course of history a clear tendency for more and more areas to become capitalized with the object of increasing their cash value. So the capitalist method of production never appears in a pure form, only as actual historical *modes of accumulation*.

> By the *accumulation process* we mean generally the organizational and technological conditions for the production of social *value*, its distribution and its re-allocation. This includes the way added value is produced (work organization, skills of the work-force, production technology: the productive factors), the volume of applied capital and its distribution into the various sectors, the length of utilization cycles, the distribution of the social product to different

classes, individual and collective (class-specific) forms and norms of consumption.[143]

But the historical realization of these factors of the accumulation process described here in general terms never comes about automatically or abstractly, but is embedded in a network of regulatory institutions.

The capitalist *regulation system* depends at its most general and abstract on the forms of socialization of the capitalist method of production: private production; the exchange of goods; the separation of capital and wage labour. The results of this are the prominence of money and the rights of citizens, competition between capitalists and between waged workers, the rise of ordinary people as formally free participants in the market and citizens, the social value given to individual choice, freedom, equality and progress. These are the basis for the *general* form and structure of regulatory institutions: the *company* as the expression of the private ownership of the means of production; the *family* as the place in society where the reproduction of the work-force, but not capitalist production, takes place; the *market*, including the labour market; *freedom of contract*; the system of private and public *rights*; the *free association* of individuals to preserve common interests (clubs, societies, employers' associations and trade unions); and the state.[144]

Regulation is accomplished in different historical interweavings of this basketwork.

Let us take as an example the case of the Fordist-Keynesian model of accumulation. In this the labour movement presses for higher wages and state intervention in social and employment policy. Out of this the capital side develops, under the general conditions of profit-bringing capitalist added value production, methods of disciplining the work-force for the sake of profit through the creation of mass-purchasing power and mass consumption.

It is important to understand that no single subject steers the process, but that individuals and groups – all driven by capital's tendency to make money through progressive capitalization – determine, through the mutual effect their behaviour has on each other, the extent to which and the form in which the interests of capital may prevail or not. Thus prepared, we shall now turn to the present-day situation in Europe within the framework of the world system.

Part II

The Capitalist European Community Single Market 1992 – and its Consequences If We Do Nothing

1. The Single European Market: Economic Consequences
2. The Single Market and the Two-thirds World
3. Division of Europe into Poor and Rich Regions
4. The Fate of Farmers in the Single Market
5. Social Questions in the Single Market
6. The Single Market and "Sustainable Development"
7. The Increasing Perversion of European Security Policy
8. Reversion to Pre-democratic Conditions or Democratization of the EC's Politics and Economy?

1. The Single European Market: Economic Consequences
Thesis 8

The Single European Market is an attempt by European owners and administrators of capital to improve their position in competition with the USA and Japan by creating the world's biggest market (340 million people), in order to increase their own opportunities for the accumulation and concentration of power. According to the official view, the four freedoms for the unhindered exchange of capital, goods, labour and services should promote prosperity for all by reducing costs.[1] In fact it is possible to foresee lower costs and higher profits for capital-owners. But this will probably lead above all to an accelerated concentration of capital and greater control of the market. As for the social and ecological costs, the satisfaction of people's basic needs and the preservation of creation, the wholly inadequate guidelines and regulations suggested so far make one fear negative consequences and great dangers. They are not fate, but must and can be fought for. It is therefore worth making clear demands, and persisting in doing so.

The European Community: a Superpower in the Making – thus wrote Johan Galtung prophetically in 1973.[2] He sums up the rise of the European Community (EC) in the basic formula: take five collapsed colonial empires, add a sixth (he means Great Britain), and make out of them all one big neo-colonial empire. That means that from its beginning after the second world war the rise of the new Europe may be seen in terms of winning back a position of power in the global political economy.

It is therefore not surprising that it was in the general view the forces of capital in the extended EC that, faced with US and Japanese competition in the world market, pushed for the completion of the Single Market. We can be relatively brief in describing these events, the structures of the EC and its consequences, actual or possible, as some excellent detailed presentations of the whole issue are readily available.[3] A few basic data will suffice here.

In 1986 the EC member states agreed on changes and extensions to the 1958 Treaty of Rome in the so-called Single European Act – with the object of completing the Single European Market by the end of 1992. The EC Commission had laid out the plans for it in 1985 in a White Paper on "Completing the Internal Market". The Act's key statement on the Single Market says:

> The Community shall adopt measures with the aim of progressively establishing the internal market over a period expiring on 31 December 1992... The internal market shall comprise an area without internal frontiers in which the free movement of goods, persons, services and capital is ensured in accordance with the provisions of this Treaty. (Art 8a)

The diagram shows what this means.[4]

THE EC ON ITS WAY TO THE SINGLE EUROPEAN MARKET
Programme for Realizing the "Four Freedoms" by the End of 1992

Free Movement of People

Abolition of border controls
Harmonisation of laws on entry,
asylum, weaopons, drugs
Freedom of settlement and
employment for EC citizens
Strengthened external controls

Free Movement of Services

Liberalisation of financial services
Harmonisation of controls on
banking and insurance
Open markets in transport and
telecommunications

Free Movement of Goods

Abolition of border controls

Harmonisation or mutual
recognition of norms and standards

Tax harmonisation

Free Movement of Capital

Greater freedom of movement for
money and capital
Steps towards a common market
for financial services
Liberalisation of traffic in
stocks and bonds

To set out the advantages of the Single Market a study was commissioned, the results of which were presented in the so-called *Cecchini report*.[5] Its core thesis is that through the abolition of bureaucratic hindrances the costs for the economy will be reduced, and thereby prosperity will be increased for all.

This neo-liberal assumption that an enlarged free market with its extended division of labour and strengthened economic growth leads automatically to prosperity for all is Adam Smith's old theory, which history has refuted a thousand times, in new clothes.[6] Under capitalist conditions the free market inevitably leads to the concentration of capital and to disadvantages to all non-owners of capital and to nature. And now, in the experience of the wave of mergers that followed the Single Market's announcement, there is clear confirmation that its first consequences are the concentration of capital and the extension of the power of the great multinationals.

Instead of the chain: cost reductions–price reductions–wider sales and thus better provisions for consumers, it is likely that profits – fluctuations caused by competition aside – will rise and that this will lead to an increase in company restructuring, rationalization, diversification, speculation and investment, and also to the further displacement and thus concentration of capital ... The former chairman of the ICI Chemicals conglomerate, Harvey-Jones, prognosticates that in the next ten years over half of the factories in Europe will be closed.[7]

The Cecchini report itself admits that, for instance, out of 16 locomotive plants only four and out of seven producers in the telecommunications sector only two will remain, though it does not reflect on this state of affairs and its consequences.[8] It is even clear that the EC is developing a body of competition law that will encourage and guide large-scale mergers and thereby push aside national law on competition and cartels.[9] It is again possible to see that the clear goal of the Single Market is to adapt to the capitalist world market's movement of capital concentration. So the key problem is again the subordination of politics to the interests of capital in the economy.

This tendency is detrimental even to the long-term interests of the economy itself. Since the 1970s the capitalist world economy has been in a structural over-accumulation crisis. That makes it increasingly difficult to invest gainfully the profits that are made, which has led to more and more dubious investment practices and crisis-provoking raids.[10]

But the main methodological error of the Cecchini report and – much worse – of the Single Market project thus far is the incorrect definition of "costs" that it leads to, and the question of how to deal with it politically. Here the "Black Paper on the Single European Market" of Heine/Kisker/Schikora (eds.) gives some first-class help on criticism and alternative action.[11] It fastens in the "Institutional Economics" tradition on to K. William Kapp's idea of "social costs".[12]

> By social costs we understand all direct and indirect charges, disadvantages or damages which third persons or the public as a whole have to bear as a result of unrestricted economic activity or political measures to encourage it. Social costs are by their content and form much more than the "external costs" of neoclassicism, which are evaluated on the basis of market data.[13]

In other words, Cecchini calculates only the costs for private companies, like an accountant, and not, like an economist, the costs for all the people, society as a whole, and nature. Yet these costs are central, not just on methodological and theoretical grounds but also if one wants to see the dangers clearly and develop strategies for action against them. This is not a matter of an abstract rejection of European union; it is to ask the question: what kind of Europe do we want – one in which the profits of banks and companies go up at any price, or a Europe in which the satisfaction of all people's basic needs (food, clothing, housing, health, work, education, socio-economic and political involvement) and a considerate attitude to nature are the guidelines? And if we want a social and ecological Europe, where are the dangers, and what are the possible political starting points from which to counter them?

For this, exemplary, particularly urgent *goals for action* should be formulated. To some extent these have already been taken up by those they affect, the trade unions or the new social movements. In part they lead directly to concrete demands to the political decision-makers; in part they may serve as bases for campaigns concerning the symbolic year 1992, as presented here in Part III.

2. The Single Market and the Two-thirds World
Thesis 9

In capitalism the weaker an actor is, the worse for him are the effects of any further strengthening of the power of capital. So potentially the biggest losers from the completion of the Single European Market are the masses and nature in the countries of the two-thirds world, the weaker among them more so than the stronger. The Single Market will clearly exacerbate the already catastrophic inequalities between the North and South and will probably sharpen even more the divergent development of the stronger "threshold countries" and the poorer "third-world countries". So far it is possible to speak only of tendencies, mainly because the EC itself and the Cecchini report consciously or unconsciously remain silent on this question. As for finance capital, it continues to extract interest from the poor in the debtor countries on the one hand and on the other hand goes, according to its nature, wherever profits beckon. The EC as such has shown itself able to go its own way on the debt question only with regard to Poland – the same must be demanded stubbornly for the countries of the two-thirds world – and is linking its financial policy even more closely to IMF conditions which create poverty. On industrial policy it is, for reasons of competition with the USA and Japan, supporting the growth of the TNCs, which for their part pursue a more aggressive policy in the world market. In trading policy the weak special measures of the Lomé regulations are being eaten up by altogether negative developments in world trade, in which the strong industrialized countries preach free trade for their products yet pursue protectionism against many products from "third-world countries". The most glaring example of this is the EC agricultural policy. In all these areas concrete goals for action, amounting ultimately to a renewed demand for a new world economic order, need to be formulated.

Even as the EC has kept quiet about the consequences of the Single Market for the countries of the two-thirds world, critical literature and the solidarity movement have with gratifying intensity occupied themselves with the theme.[14] It is, admittedly, not yet possible to describe exactly and quantify the consequences that are anticipated. One is compelled methodologically to speak of tendencies that may be extrapolated from the status quo.

With regard to *finance capital* we must address first, as the tip of the iceberg, the debt crisis. A distinction should be made here between European commercial banks, governments and the EC. The banks are still following the tough course of exacting interest from the poor, which in 1990 led to a net capital transfer of over 50 billion US dollars from the South to the rich North. Since the solidarity campaigns of 1988 the governments and the EC have not excluded a reduction of the debts of the poorest countries; but, in view of the other factors in the world economic system which tend to make them poorer, this has brought about no fundamental change for these countries, above all because the EC generally tends to tie any remission to the IMF's and the world market's idea of good economic and political behaviour. The only really new prospect is in the fifty percent reduction of Poland's debt, which is obviously politically motivated. From this follows

Action goal 1:

In view of five hundred years of colonial and neo-colonial robbery, the EC member states should in 1992 remit the debts of the debtor countries in order, according to Susan George's model of debt release, to give them a chance to initiate, with the involvement of popular organizations of the poor, their own form of socio-economic and ecological development.[15]

But measures of this kind will still be only patchwork unless the general conditions and institutions of the world economic system are changed fundamentally. In terms of the international financial system the crucial thing is to democratize the plutocratically organized IMF and World Bank and make them accountable to all the countries that play a part in the world economy. So Section II of the WCC assembly at Canberra was right to make the demand that the UN and the International Court of Justice be given more power. Because the US dollar has in fact lost its strength as an undisputed leading currency, and the European currency, the ECU, will in the future play (like the Yen) an equal role, Europe has the opportunity to revise what the USA laid down at Bretton Woods in 1944 and call for a more just financial system. That there are more just alternatives has already been shown by the proposal by Keynes that was not accepted at Bretton Woods.[16] From this follows:

Action goal 2:

The European governments and the EC should work for the development of a new international financial system in which not just debtors but also creditors have to bear the burdens of adjustment. For this the IMF and the World Bank must be fundamentally democratized and made accountable to all participant countries. A first step towards this could be support for the "Reform or Dismantle the Bretton Woods Institutions Now" campaign, which is supported by the Latin American and Caribbean Councils of Churches.[17]

But since finance capital is organized transnationally and is thus constantly striving to free itself from national and international political control, it is also important to use legislation as far as possible to stop the banks extending their power even more by means of the Single Market – something that can already be observed. The heart of the question is whether the universal banking system will prevail as in Germany. This means that banks can be savings banks, credit banks and investment banks, all at the same time. It leads to a situation where the commercial banks are able in practice to pack the boards of companies and run the real economy in their own interest.

Action goal 3:

In the capital sector the (universal) banks should be prevented by legislation from controlling both finance and industrial capital. It should be insisted that a division of powers and democratic control is brought into economic life as well.

In the area of *industrial capital* the EC, as I have shown, is encouraging concentration in order to improve its competitive position against the USA and Japan. Indirectly this encourages more offensive and aggressive activity by European TNCs in the world market, and the countries of the two-thirds world have scarcely any power against it. This will lead naturally, on the one hand, to more strenuous technological efforts to replace raw materials by synthetic products. On the other hand, TNCs will withdraw production facilities from those countries and set them up in cheap-wage areas in Europe. Thus many poor countries will be barred from the production sector against their will, and their people made "surplus" – perhaps able still to act as receivers of waste, especially poisoned waste, from the rich.[18]

Action goal 4:

Although by a basic assumption of the capitalist system control over transnational companies is in the last analysis impossible, the least that should be demanded is tougher laws on cartels, in order to have at least some influence over price manipulation.

In the area of *trading capital* and trade institutions the states of Africa, the Caribbean and the Pacific (the ACP states) have been able through the Lomé Agreement to get special conditions, as demanded in the discussions on a new world economic order in the 1970s: "At Lomé the EC did not just give up the principle of counter-preferences and accept a duty to open its markets, it also made available means of finance to compensate for the loss of exports because of severe fluctuations in raw materials prices (Stabex) and for the reorganizing of mining companies (Sysmin)."[19] Yet in the fourth Lomé extension the EC excluded many agricultural products and semi-finished and finished goods from the Agreement. That applies even more to non-associated countries, for which just the normal GATT regulations apply. And these have one single goal: freedom of trade for the strong and protectionism against the weak. On the whole it is true to say "that the EC today is already fencing off its markets against products that it is unable to produce competitively itself and/or is trying to prevent the emergence of potential new competitors".[20] On top of this Lomé IV forces participating ACP states to follow the structural adjustment policies of the IMF.

Action goal 5:

The EC must be challenged to extend the Lomé regulations into a new, fair world economic system for all countries and not to do away with them. It must also be challenged to change the rules of GATT which now mean "free trade for the strong – protectionism against the weak" towards affirmative action for the weaker participants in world trade.

Perhaps the most negative area of EC policy in terms of its social costs, which the Single Market will further increase, is agricultural policy. It affects not only the two-thirds world but also European farmers and consumers. Before we turn to this, however, we must take a quick look at the effects of the Single European Market on the different regions of Europe.

3. Division of Europe into Poor and Rich Regions

Thesis 10

The profit-oriented logic of capital exploits in ever subtler ways the weaknesses not just of individual economic subjects but also of the different regions. That leads, not just with regard to the two-thirds world but also in Europe itself, to a layered hierarchy of winners and losers – both between countries and within individual countries. Particularly disadvantaged are Southern Europe and Ireland. The Single Market will sharpen these disparities. The EC regional policy we now have is inadequate to correct this, and must be greatly strengthened. Developing the countries of Central and Eastern Europe presents a problem of a very special and particularly difficult kind.

Just as it is insufficient to talk of the division between the "first" and "third" world because divisions between and within the countries of the two-thirds world are becoming ever more marked, so it is in Europe too. The Single Market will sharpen regional differences between richer and poorer countries of the EC as much as between the EC and other European countries – and regional disparities in individual countries as well.[21] Even empirical studies commissioned by the EC Commission have had to admit: "It is impossible to overstress the fact that the rich regions of Europe have become richer and the poor poorer."[22] And this trend will be reinforced by the Single Market. The reason for this is the strengthening of the market power of the banks and corporations, which are able to use to their advantage the Single Market's international division of labour.

> These processes of concentration in the course of further internationalization lead to the cementing of regional inequalities in that they bring about the further location of central company units in those areas that grew with the rising challenge of highly complex large-scale production. These are above all the developed regions of countries that are already economically dominant... The peripheral regions are brought in mainly through a kind of international division of labour by locating there labour-intensive component production units which exploit the cost of relatively unskilled labour and have hardly any symbiosis with the locality. As a rule these branch plants induce neither structural improvements nor above-average growth rates. Frequently they are never able to compensate for the loss of traditional sectors.[23]

The EC has tried since 1975 to respond to this problem, at first with the European Regional Development Fund, which was later complemented by other structural funds. The Single European Act of 1987 then caused them to be topped up further. But these structural funds are in no way adequate, and cannot tackle the increasingly divisive effects of the Single Market. At the moment we have a welcome object lesson on what happens when two economies of different strengths are tied together in a "free" market: the example of the German Democratic Republic after the economic and currency union. Here the additional problem of changing from a planned economy to a market economy presents a further complication, but many phenomena will probably be similar when borders are abolished in the Single Market. That is because national governments will have hardly any opportunity to control things.

> In the event structurally weak regions are in danger of being drawn into the international division of labour as marginalized sub-contractor regions, without any regard for their regional specialities and development potential.[24]

Here too, of course, we still have no final picture. Yet we can already say with certainty the following:

Action goal 6:

The EC must decisively improve its Regional Fund and above all develop with the present national states instruments to counteract division within the individual countries.

Sweden's inclusion in the Single Market will be interesting. In all probability the "Swedish model" of a developed social state will die. On the other hand it will be interesting to see whether the entry of a country with a relatively strong social orientation in both domestic and foreign policy will be able to strengthen the EC's social component.

The effect of the Single Market on the countries and economies of Central and Eastern Europe and the Soviet Union presents a special problem of particular consequence. We cannot simply set it aside, for a whole host of unknowns are in play here. However, we can take as a comparison for throwing light on possible tendencies the model of the behaviour of the industrialized countries and the EC towards the so-called newly industrialized countries, if not towards the "developing countries", above all because their high debts are comparable. Here too the heart of the relationship will probably be exploitation of the international division of labour by the transnational banks and corporations.

An example: The Soviet Union is rich in minerals – raw materials under the conditions of the world market – that interests the West. The EC Commission is therefore in the process of drawing up an "Energy Charter" for contracts by Western countries with the States of the former USSR. "The Charter will lay down basic principles like free access to energy sources for investors, the protection of investments, including the repatriation of profits in hard currency, the free exchange of technological know-how under the protection of licences on patents and a 'right of transit' using existing or future distribution networks for electricity, natural gas and oil."[25] In plain language: the USSR as a supplier of raw materials to the West on terms whereby the oil companies rake off the Soviet energy industry's profits with the enticement that it could earn hard currency. The Greens in the European Parliament rightly criticized this for "exploiting the Soviet Union, creating work for the West European nuclear industry, and destroying yet again chances for decentralized energy and heating".[26]

It means that the basic tendency with regard to Eastern Europe and the Soviet Union will be their division into regions that get richer and regions that get poorer – to say nothing at all about divisions within these countries between groups of winners and losers. To these we shall turn now.

4. The Fate of Farmers in the Single Market
Thesis 11

The capitalization of agriculture has led to its industrialization and to the transnational agro-business, which results not only in hunger in the two-thirds world but also in driving farms (apart from big industrial ones) into debt and destroying them, in the progressive degradation of the land's natural basis, in dangers to the health of consumers and, specially in the EC, in the fleecing of taxpayers. This state of affairs is well known. It is equally well known who profits from this: agro-business, the banks and the big industrial farmers. Here, as in hardly any other area, there are clear alternative proposals. The "Aachen Declaration" is a summary of such proposals.

If there is one open scandal in the policies of the EC, it is in the area of agriculture. So far there is no sign at all that plans for the Single Market will change anything; on the contrary, there is reason to fear that the present disastrous development will become even worse.[27] There are clear analyses of this state of affairs, with alternative proposals as well, concisely summarized in the "Aachen Declaration". Instead of making my own presentation I shall reproduce it here:[28]

Aachen Declaration, 2 July 1987

Farmers and consumers for a new agricultural policy

...The picture most people have is that the Commission in Brussels is not getting a grip on the agriculture problem but is squandering enormous sums on subsidies which ostensibly flow into the farmers' pockets. In reality the agricultural policy has specifically encouraged overproduction. The subsidies go essentially not to the farmers but to adjacent areas, the food industry, food retailing and export companies. These exercise a significant influence on the structure of agriculture.

For two years there has been talk of reform of the agricultural policy. Virtually unnoticed by the general public, a policy has been sharpened up which could lead within a few years to the destruction of farming as we know it... The present agricultural policy does nothing to remove the causes of our present evils but makes the problems even worse. Therefore, for the first time in the history of the Federal Republic of Germany, farmers', environmental, consumer and development organizations got together in order to set against the Brussels policy demands for a new agricultural policy which is social, ecological and concerned with the needs of all.

Effects of the agricultural policy of the EC and the German government

... on agriculture

The EC agricultural policy has led to the destruction of the livelihoods of small and medium-sized farmers...

... on the environment

The compulsion to grow or fail has led to more and more intensive cultivation, with often dramatic consequences for the environment and nature...

... on the consumer

It is a mark of the way in which our food is provided that fewer and fewer products come direct to the consumer. In recent decades the food industry and food wholesalers have intervened more and more between the farmer and the consumer. Increasingly agricultural products have become mere raw materials for industry and trade...

... on the third world

The European Community has become an overproducer of the most important agricultural products. The EC is the world's second biggest exporter and biggest importer of agricultural goods. Only imports of food, agricultural raw materials and animal feed, mostly from third-world countries, make overproduction in Western

Europe possible. Without these imports the EC would not even be able to provide enough food for itself.

The heavy subsidies on EC agricultural exports have led to price penetration all over the world. For example, third-world producers suffer severe losses on sugar exports. The domestic markets of many third-world states have been breached through the aggressive export policies of the EC and the USA...

The EC, therefore, is responsible for the one-sided alignment of agriculture in these supplier-countries on a few kinds of production for export, the increasing suppression of food production for domestic use, the destruction of small-scale farming and the reckless exploitation of the environment.

By its market regulation policy the EC fences off its own markets against very many agricultural goods and competitive producers...

Whom does the agricultural policy benefit?

The consumers are given the picture by the media that the farmers profit from the subsidies. The farmers are told again and again that the consumers should enjoy favourable food prices. Both estimations divert attention from the real beneficiaries.

The present agricultural policy benefits the chemicals industry, the farm machinery industry, the banks, above all the big boys in the food industry, the food wholesalers, and import/export companies.

For a new agricultural policy

The EC Commission's thinking in the "Green Paper" of July 1985 and the resultant proposals for price reductions are aimed directly at the farmers. The object of the EC agricultural policy is finally to get rid of traditional farming and put factory-farming in its place...

The need for adequate and healthy food throughout the world must regain more recognition. Human needs must be given more weight than economic criteria...

A new agricultural policy for farmers

A future agricultural policy must enable the farmers to stay in agriculture. Farms should not be run on normal management principles (maximization of profits). Agriculture must serve the whole of society...

(Action goal 7):

The most important thing is that work on farms is properly paid. To take account of regional differences and differing production costs, we demand the introduction of a system of graduated prices for producers that will secure livings for small and medium-scale farmers. With milk, for example, all farmers producing more than 200,000 litres should be paid 10 Pfennig per litre extra for the first 60,000 litres.

To remove surpluses and reduce industrialized animal husbandry, we demand stock limits related to land area (60 milch-cows, 240 beef cattle, 100 breeding sows, 800 porkers).

A new agricultural policy for nature

Besides the production of healthy food, agriculture is of central importance for maintaining the land and the variety of animal and plant species...

(Action goal 8):

An end to the growing structural loss among small and medium- scale farmers, and measures to maintain small and medium-scale farming rather than specialized large-scale farming.

Reduction of surpluses by the generally reduced use of fertilizers and insecticides.

Linking cattle numbers to land area (stock limits).

A ban on substances agreed to be environmentally harmful, like Atrazine, Lindane, etc., and tougher secondary controls on food quality.

Plans to "set aside" land (and farms) and programmes for the even more intensive use of productive land for alcohol production to be rejected.

Massive promotion of organic production methods.

An end to the continued building-over of great tracts of land.

A new agricultural policy for the consumer

The agricultural policy must guarantee that the population is provided with high-quality, cheap food at minimum disturbance to the balance of nature. So we demand:

(Action goal 9):

A halt to the process of concentration in food production and distribution.

The decentralization of distribution.

The decentralization of dairies and abbatoirs.

The abolition of trading regulations which emphasize optical characteristics and storage time.

The abolition of all so-called quality standards which serve not the product's health value but the requirements of the industry that produces it.

The encouragement of direct marketing, particularly by consumers'/producers' cooperatives.

The encouragement of food crafts.

The establishment of independent institutions for control and advice.

A new European agricultural policy for the third world

With regard to a proper concern for the interest of people in the third world, we call upon the EC to reorient its agricultural policy. It should not build upon a worldwide agricultural division of labour, in which the third-world countries are in effect reduced to being replaceable suppliers of agricultural raw materials. By the same token the third world should not be used as a market for off-loading processed foods from Europe. A European agricultural policy must give precedence to the right of all countries to secure their own basis of nourishment.

(Action goal 10):

There must be no replacement of agricultural goods by exports.

The EC's surplus production should be reduced by promoting and supporting traditional agriculture.

During the next year food aid should be reduced to pure emergency aid and should as far as possible be provided exclusively from surpluses in the third world (triangular trading).

EC imports, particularly of animal feed, may be reduced by having less factory-farming. In cases where there are relationships of dependence of a significantly one-sided kind, the EC should be responsible for bearing the cost of resultant structural deficits and making equalization payments.

In particular the EC's imports of animal feed must be reduced step by step over the next few years. The liberalization of the world feed trade sought for in the GATT negotiations should be rejected. The reduction of feed imports should be regulated by bilateral trade agreements with each supplier country. The EC should, out of its shared responsibility for the structural problems created in these countries, make compensation payments to give them scope to re-orient their economies on their domestic markets.

Agricultural goods should be traded only when each country has met its own needs for basic foodstuffs and on the basis of a varied production structure. They should be exported only when this is meaningful in terms of development politics (and when most food is self-provided) for the overall economic development of the country concerned. In such cases better access to the EC's agro-market must be created.

Agriculture in Western Europe stands at a decisive turning-point. There are still real chances of avoiding the worst, the wholesale destruction of traditional farming and the total industrialization of agricultural production. To prevent this and to open new prospects for the men and women who work on the land, all those who are aware of the issue must close ranks. Therefore, we call upon all concerned organizations and individuals to support this declaration and to join the struggle for an agriculture which is social and ecological, which shows solidarity with all, and which serves the countries of the third world, nature, the farmer and the consumers.

* * * *

If the picture drawn by the "Aachen Declaration" is correct, that the transnational economic system in general and the EC in particular disadvantage the farmers (except the big ones), are the winners those who work in industry?

5. Social Questions in the Single Market
Thesis 12

Behind the fact that the Single Market is coming into being in the context of neo-liberal capitalism lurks the danger that its social elements will get even weaker. The results are mass unemployment and "poverty in prosperity". Official EC trust in the Cecchini report's view of the employment effects of economic growth and the market is refuted by the facts. The active elements of EC social policy like the Social Charter suffer from having no legal force, and anyway affect only employees. They offer no solution to the problem of structural unemployment. Particularly badly hit are women, young people, migrant workers and refugees. The rapid and effective internationalizing of trade unions and social movements is vital for the creation of counter-pressure.

When we consider the social questions of the Single Market it is important to remind ourselves of the world economic conditions in which we at present operate. Neo-liberal, monetarist capitalism is trying, under the slogans of "deregulation" and "the free market", to dismantle all the elements of the social state left from the Keynesian phase. The result is mass unemployment and "poverty in prosperity".[29] What effect has the Single Market on this general trend?

We shall look first at the situation of *working people*.[30]

If we are to believe the Cecchini report, after a short-term increase in unemployment a positive effect in job terms is to be expected. The basis for this view is the methodologically questionable assumption that economic growth creates jobs. But the 1980s showed that companies use growth to enable rationalization and take-overs, which destroy jobs. In the Single Market this tendency will naturally be felt more in weak industries and regions, less in strong ones. A further problem is the neglect of the effects of monetary policy in the Cecchini report, which assumes a tendency towards lower interest rates – something else that the facts contradict.[31]

Hope rests, therefore, on the EC's active *social policy*. The 1985 White Paper on the Single Market contains nothing on social policy and the Cecchini report just as little. Yet the Single European Act, which came into force in 1987, included in the extension of the EEC Treaty in article 118a the possibility that minimum requirements in the field of the working environment might be determined by a qualified majority in the Council of Ministers. This shows that the EC can also decide on social improvements if there is enough pressure, and in any case there is no need to fear automatic "social dumping".

In 1989 the heads of state and government of the EC member states decided on the "Community Charter of the Fundamental Social Rights of Workers" (normally shortened to "Social Charter", as opposed to the Council of Europe's "European Social Charter").[32] D. Beckmann *et al.* put this as follows:

> The Social Charter, which had to be rewritten constantly because of the rigorous opposition of the British government, disappointed the expectations of the trade unions above all and of the European Parliament. The trade unions' demand for a mandatory, Europe-wide floor of basic social rights, to prevent social dumping and enable a progressive social development in Europe, was not fulfilled. In the view of its critics the document presents a collection of non-binding principles and neither specifies precisely minimum social norms nor pays the slightest attention to the demand that they be mandatory. By anchoring it in the principle of subsidiarity, which expressly accepts common

action only when something cannot be handled at national level, responsibility in social matters is at virtually every step handed back to the governments of the member states. This fact above all frustrates hopes of common action in European social policy.[33]

In practical terms social dumping means that with different social policies in the individual member states transnational corporations can reduce their costs by choosing the socially cheapest location. In 1989 the Commission submitted in addition a social action programme. But even here only 19 out of 45 initiatives contain proposals for binding EC norms.[34] So as yet neither the Social Charter nor the action programme is adequate to prevent social dumping.

A further field is rights of participation or co-determination in companies located in more than one country. Here as well regulations intended to be mandatory have failed before the Council of Ministers and the resistance of employers. Even the so-called social dialogue is still non-mandatory. Out of this emerges

Action goal 11:

> To prevent social dumping in the Single European Market, binding common rights throughout Europe, which lay down minimum social standards and secure participation rights for workers, must be created under the intervention of the European Parliament and with the backing of the European Court of Justice. It need not involve fully-unified European legislation, but must at all events provide a framework "which prevents the dismantling of social rights and achievements and supports the progressive development of social standards in Europe."[35]

There is a particular problem in the fact that, whilst companies are organized truly transnationally, the trade unions are only starting out on European cooperation. Worldwide cooperation is even weaker, so workers throughout the world can easily be played off against one another. This being so, the continuing development of European social policy, which for its part must be firmly bedded in the struggle for worldwide justice, depends crucially on the internationalization of the trade union movement.

The greatest weakness of the Social Charter is that it applies only to those in work.[36] But what are its effects on those who, because of unemployment or other reasons, do not come under protection for workers? Here we must raise not just the question of social benefits and social programmes but the question of the legitimacy of structural unemployment in general. Unemployment is made. Through unemployment industry makes money, and on top of that it can use it to discipline workers. The psychological effects on the unemployed are devastating, so structural unemployment helps break down solidarity among working people and in society as a whole. Here again the basic question is this: How is the added value we create shared? Instead of increasing profits it is possible to go for work-sharing and therefore shorter hours. Instead of paying benefits, the state can invest in a policy of employment. Unemployment exists only because the people accept it.

Action goal 12:

> By means of publicity by the unemployed, the trade unions and the new social movements it must be made clear to the national and European institutions that an economy which produces structural unemployment is politically impracticable. This demand should be made concrete in law and employment policy.

Women have particular reasons for fear.[37] Early on (1975 onwards) the EC decided on guidelines for the equal treatment of men and women. All of them concerned employed work and were to that extent motivated by not just humanitarian but also economic considerations: they were to prevent the distortion of competition in the different European countries in the event of companies exploiting bad conditions for women in any one of them.[38] No country has really translated these guidelines into valid legislation – least of all Germany – so that women have had frequently to go to the European Court.[39] Within the EC an active women's policy could be really promoted.

In fact, there is no real concept of a policy for women beyond this equality policy which is economically motivated. In work itself women suffer from the fact that they are particularly affected by the division between regular work and part-time work, home work and flexible work.[40] In addition, a disproportionately large number of women and young people fall victim to unemployment. From all these follows

Action goal 13:

> The EC must expand its active women's policy decisively and above all take care that its fundamentals are set in the legal form of ordinances binding on the member states, not in the non-binding form of guidelines; for the freedoms of the Single Market have an inbuilt tendency to work to the disadvantage of those who are weakest.

The weakest among the victims, however, are probably *migrant workers and refugees* – and amongst them again women, children and the elderly (though there will also be within the Single Market an increased migration of skilled workers, managers, etc., whom we can bracket out here). It is important to distinguish between the groups concerned: migrant workers, refugees and – particularly in the case of Germany – migrants of German origin from the ex-GDR and Central and Eastern Europe. In the case of migrant workers we must again make a distinction between those from countries within the EC and those from outside.[41]

Those from EC member states are not the real problem group; they enjoy relatively favourable conditions, which the Single Market should further improve.[42] All of them, of course, share the social problems, indicated above, of workers in a capitalist market. But the worst hit are foreign workers from outside the EC; for such migrants have only second-class rights.[43] They depend on legislation and the vagaries of the market in individual states; they have hardly any social security rights; and their ability to bring their families with them is restricted. Since the recession at the beginning of the 1970s the restrictions have become increasingly tough.

The same applies to policy on refugees and asylum. Here the picture some have drawn of a "fortress Europe" is justified. Legislation is marked increasingly by the wish to frighten off, exclude and discriminate.[44] But particularly disturbing is the fact that, in the main, EC policy on asylum and refugees is not being made by legally constituted bodies but by committees that work in secret, set up by different groups of member countries, chiefly the Schengen Group (originally Belgium, Netherlands, Luxembourg, France, Germany), the TREVI Groups (all 12 member states) and the Ad Hoc Group on Immigration (Home Secretaries of the 12).[45] The 1985 Schengen Agreement dealt mainly with definitions of the free movement of goods, services and people between the signatory states. But in 1990 it was expanded by an additional agreement that contained the following new points:

1) measures to strengthen external borders;
2) a common policy on visas;
3) a common policy on refugees and asylum;
4) the setting-up of a data bank known as the Schengen Information System (SIS).[46]

The frightening-off system is complemented by the TREVI Groups, which use the same means to deal with drug-dealers, terrorists and international organized crime on the one hand and illegal immigrants, refugees and asylum-seekers on the other.[47] In both cases the EC Commission has no right to participate, or officially to information – not to mention the fact that the European Parliament has no possibility of legislating and the public no chance of engaging in democratic discussion.

Any consideration of the shared responsibility of Europe and the West for the causes of migration and the misery of refugees is completely out of the question.

> This applies not only to the colonial heritage and the results of the colonialist policies of many EC states, which have led in the third world to processes of impoverishment, civil wars and hunger, but also to their contribution to the "restitutive modernization" of third-world states, which has helped turn people into potential or real migrant workers. Through their massive exports of weapons which have been deployed in the third world the Western industrial countries have played at least an indirect part in the creation of the streams of refugees.[48]

Nothing shows the Western system's similarity to the *system of apartheid* as clearly as the issue of migration and refugees. Like the whites in

South Africa, the Western industrialized nations, including Western Europe as a whole, divide up the world's resources and labour in their own interest, but deny them access to the "white areas" and their plundered abundance. The long-term answer to the problem of migrants and refugees is therefore the destruction of world apartheid, i.e. the development of a new world economic system which leaves for the societies of the two-thirds world the resources they need to meet their people's basic needs. That leads us to

Action goal 14:

Bearing in mind its direct and indirect responsibility for the causes of migration and the misery of refugees, the EC must be brought to the point of taking on, through its legal organs, full responsibility for a humane policy on migration and asylum. The arrangements introduced undemocratically by the Schengen and TREVI Groups to scare off, shut out and discriminate against foreigners from non-EC countries must be revised. So the question of a new world economic system must also be placed on the EC's agenda, for only in this way can the causes of migration and the misery of refugees be tackled.

6. The Single Market and "Sustainable Development"
Thesis 13

The European environment groups have made a critique of the Single Market and drawn up a catalogue of concrete demands which are worthy of support. The project of "sustainable development" is set against the concept of economic growth and profit with its consequence of ecological dumping. The concept is made concrete in proposals on energy, traffic, agriculture, waste and chemicals, on regional policy and tourism, and in demands for laws, taxes and a right of information. The crucial question of West-East and North-South relations also makes one conclude that a new social and ecological world economic order is urgently needed.

In none of the areas touched by the Single Market does opposition seem so well organized as in that of the environment. In March 1991 the European Environment Office, the association of European environmental groups, presented a comprehensive White Paper on an ecological economic policy for the EC entitled "The Single European Market and the Environment".[49] The authors start from evidence "that through the Single Market there will be unleashed or at least strengthened wrong developments which will in the next few decades make the environmental situation dramatically worse" (p.5). They identify as design errors in the Single Market programme the following six points (pp.5f.):

1. The EC 1992 project builds on an unbroken optimism over growth and technology. The main object is to raise growth rates, not the introduction of

"sustainable development". The policy we have so far will not suffice to make development less intensive in energy and raw materials. A projection of present trends indicates significant mid-term growth in the following areas: carbon dioxide emissions (+ 48% by 2010), road traffic (up to 77% by 2010), air traffic (approx. 100% by 2000), special waste, use of paper, and electricity consumption. These are signs of a wasteful path of development.

2. This is connected with the accountancy-led philosophy of the Single Market project. The means of completing the Single Market follow the accountancy maxims of lowest possible production costs. Yet in the area of environmental protection, faith in markets that function without friction proves groundless.

Without incentives and limiting conditions, companies are forced in a market economy to pass ecological and social costs on to the public. In many areas the efficient use of scarce natural resources contradicts the maxims of low factory production costs. Transport, energy and waste management are examples of this. Programmes to internalize these costs through market instruments, incentives, bans, too, are mostly put off in the EC.

3. In the EC, market integration has priority over political integration. Plans to liberalize the various markets are put out first – and only later does a common policy follow. A policy like that can only run after the environmental problems it itself creates. Many measures to shape limiting conditions happen, if at all, years too late, after structural change has evoked the threat of traffic collapse, the emergency in waste management or the greenhouse effect.

4. The Single Market programme settles one-sidedly on reducing costs by mass production. This brings the danger that ecological and cultural variety will be lost in the unification tendency of mass production by worldwide companies. The innovative potential of regional and local differences, regionalized markets and also regional differences on environmental policy is systematically ignored in favour of unifying tendencies. This can only be an obstacle for progress on environmental policy, since European standards have mostly lagged behind the international standard, and it has become even harder for countries to set the pace on product-related environmental policy and also energy and transport policy.

5. The EC still backs large-scale, high-risk technologies. This choice of technologies, which threatens to be reinforced by the Single Market and is being massively promoted politically, is inefficient in ecological terms and risky: this applies above all to nuclear and genetic technology.

6. The central reason why liberalization and harmonization are out of phase, why ideas on environmental policy are so scarce and why the stress is on high-risk technologies lies in the one-sidedness of the interests represented and the EC's institutional weakness. The EC is still profoundly undemocratic. Politics in the EC is still done in the tradition of the secret diplomacy of foreign policy, not according to the basic concepts of democratic power-sharing. Environmental politics in the EC still happens mainly in the closed circles of the national bureaucracies and the European Commission, and in the industrial lobbies concerned. The Council of Ministers itself often blocks things and is thought to be anxious not to give up too many of its competences to a democratically legitimized body like the European Parliament.

Against this the environmental groups place the concept of "sustainable development".[50] To put this across they formulate seven principles:

1) the priority of political integration over economic integration in Europe;

2) new criteria for economic development (replacing the growth goal with the goal of "sustainable development");

3) the integration of environmental policy into other sectors (by EC committees and authorities as well as national governments);

4) the principle of subsidiarity (in a double sense as the right of the lowest level to the best environmental policy and as a new form of cooperation among all political levels in order to increase the possibilities of action for the lowest levels and improve efficiency at all levels);

5) the "polluter pays" principle (ecological duties and taxes; extension of criminal liability; etc.);

6) the precaution principle (balancing the risk of a – possibly wrong – intervention against the risk of too late action).

The environmental groups also make detailed proposals for laws, taxes and duties, for a right to information and for change in the areas of energy, transport, agriculture, waste prevention, regional policy and tourism. They hope for a positive stimulus to EC policy from the entry of the European Free Trade Association countries, but they see dangers in the development of Central and Eastern Europe in that the cost of development is being played off against priority for the environment. It is important to oppose resolutely the exploitation of the East's economic weakness by dumping there Western civilization's rubbish. With regard to the two-thirds world they demand that responsibility be transferred from GATT to the UN economic organization, UNCTAD, with the following five main demands:

1) the cancellation of public and private debts;

2) the ecologically-oriented reshaping of Western credit policy;

3) a new ecological world economic system;

4) agrarian reform and new town-country relationships in many third-world countries;

5) the securing of human rights for threatened peoples in the rain forests.

This is a convincing programme. Therefore we may summarize it in

Action goal 15:

The principles and demands of the European environment groups in the White Paper on "The Single European Market and the Environment" should be whole-heartedly supported.

7. The Increasing Perversion of European Security Policy
Thesis 14

According to the Intelligence Conference of (North and South) American Armies (CEA), this world system's final reality is the battle for "the domination and distribution of natural resources and of strategic raw materials". After the failure of the Great War To Attain Victory in Vietnam, the USA developed Low Intensity Conflict (LIC) to secure the West's leading position of power. With the Soviet Union's realignment with the West, Mid-Intensity Conflict (MIC) in the South is once more possible, as the Gulf War shows.

With lightning speed this war so strengthened the long-latent tendency to give the EC a military arm that a West European Rapid Deployment Force for wars against the South now seems a certainty. At the same time the arms industry and its exports are experiencing a rapid upswing. Internally there is developing – hardly noticed by the public and beyond the influence of the European Parliament – an enormous surveillance system, not only to defend fortress Europe against foreigners but embracing European citizens as well.

Western Europe and in particular Germany face a decision as to whether, together and in competition with the USA (which in the twentieth century until now did most of the West's imperialist dirty work), they should on the five hundredth anniversary of Europe's securing dominion of the world by force become an openly colonialist superpower once more, or after the end of the East-West conflict contribute to a world order for justice, peace and the integrity of creation.

In capitalism arms and war have a double meaning, as became clear already at the beginning of the European world system. On the one hand capital can be accumulated easily and quickly for the arms industry and its suppliers at the tax-payers' cost, as Rosa Luxemburg saw clearly.[51] Especially in times of recession capitalist powers react with wars, as can be shown from the history of the USA since the second world war.[52] On the other hand, arms and war are part of an overall strategy in a conflict over "the domination and distribution of natural resources and of strategic raw materials", as the secret services of the American military put it in a secret paper of 1987.[53] As I have shown above, this strategy is graduated into warfare of low and mid-intensity and also into full-scale war with ABC weapons of mass destruction. That became impossible because of Gorbachev's peace policy. But precisely because of this, the USA was able not only to pursue its low-intensity war undisturbed but also to put into practice in the Gulf war the mid-intensity strategy it had been developing since 1988.[54] This strategy, as I have said, is directed against rising states of the two-thirds world, which become, with the help of Western technology, so strong that they are able to exercise pressure at a strategic point on the world economy which the West controls.

With astonishing speed the experience of this war accelerated and strengthened tendencies towards a common EC security policy in the sense of the imperialist exhibition of power. Until then EC security policy stood in the tension between the concepts of "the European pillar of NATO" (US position) and the "European security union" (driving force: France, increasingly Germany as well; curbing force: Ireland, Denmark and Greece).[55] Now the Single European Act, together with the Single Market, has undoubtedly turned the waverers in the direction of a political union which includes security policy. This parallel development will certainly continue as is proved by the consequences, in this respect, of the Gulf war. At the same time there was talk of forcing the setting up of a Rapid Deployment Force for use against countries of the two-thirds world in the framework of NATO and of also of an independent West European security policy.

Here I see great danger. If present trends persist, situations will be created which leave the citizens of Europe with a choice only between the plague and cholera. They will have either to pay for US-led mercenary armies against the South or do the imperialist dirty work themselves – certainly, if they do, by means of Low Intensity Conflict, as the disclosures about the secret NATO "Gladio" unit show. In particular, Germany would become involved in this master-plan through changes introduced in her constitution. Through a West European defence union she would also share in the decision-making on nuclear weapons, which was till now legally prohibited because of her own renunciation. Again (imperialist) war would start from German soil. Psychological warfare and opinion manipulation during the Gulf war and after it already show their impact. And all of that is happening without democratic legitimation, since in this affair the European Parliament (still) has no authority.

It seems to me crucial for the European peace and social movements, together with the trade unions and churches, to fight this democratically unlegitimated rise of militarism and imperialism. The German people showed before the Gulf war that from the experience of the second world war they prefer majority, peaceful solutions to conflicts. Movements, trade unions and churches can build on that. The goal must be: pan-European systems of mutual security in the framework of a reformed UN peace order that outlaws war. That leads to

Action goal 16:

We must stop Europe's development into a militaristic, imperialist Great Power with the help of a Rapid Deployment Force to secure the Single Market's interests in opposition to the South and Europe's cooperation in this connection with US strategies of Low and Mid-Intensity Conflict, and instead call for a pan-European system of mutual security in association with the CSCE and a reform of UNO to achieve the worldwide outlawing of war and a global order for peace. Arms exports to the outside world by EC member states must be banned by law.

The security question concerns not just the EC's foreign policy but also its domestic policy. In Western Europe, I presume, no-one would dare to write, as the authors of the Santa Fe II document did when Bush entered office, a policy paper[56] which defines the social content of democracy as freedom of enterprise and the capital market (as the core of social freedom). As politically democratic institutions, elected governments are regarded, because of their limited period of office, as "temporary governments"; the "permanent apparatus of government" of the military, the civil bureaucracy and the police and judiciary is moved into first place as the true expression of democratic control. In Europe this will not be said openly at top levels where they like to talk of the high ideals of freedom and democracy. But in reality European politics runs exactly the same way. The core is market freedom. Politically the parliament plays a wholly subordinate role, and the bureaucracy – and increasingly the police and judiciary – have plenary powers which become increasingly stronger.

We have already come across this question in connection with the walling off of Fortress Europe against foreigners. But the Single Market's planned freedom of movement for persons has also made police and judicial authorities work hard together on plans to tighten up *internal security*, as the diagram on page 66 shows.[57]

It should not be disputed here that the police have to make provisions for the new situation of the Single Market. On the question of foreigners, however, several points give cause for alarm and vigilance. Included under terrorism are also the independence struggles of British-occupied Northern Ireland and the Basques. In the old West Germany, and certainly today as well, anyone who does not have a positive relation to the Bundeswehr could and can be checked out by internal security intelligence. The ecumenical assembly for "Peace with Justice" in Basel in 1989 was watched closely by the Swiss secret service. The activities of the secret NATO "Gladio" unit have already been mentioned. If we take into account the building-up, with the most modern technology, of a European information service, we become aware of a clear tendency towards the increasing surveillance, outside democratic control, of European citizens. Hence

Action goal 17:

The development of systems of internal security in the EC must be democratically controlled and restricted by law.

66 Europe in the World System 1492 – 1992

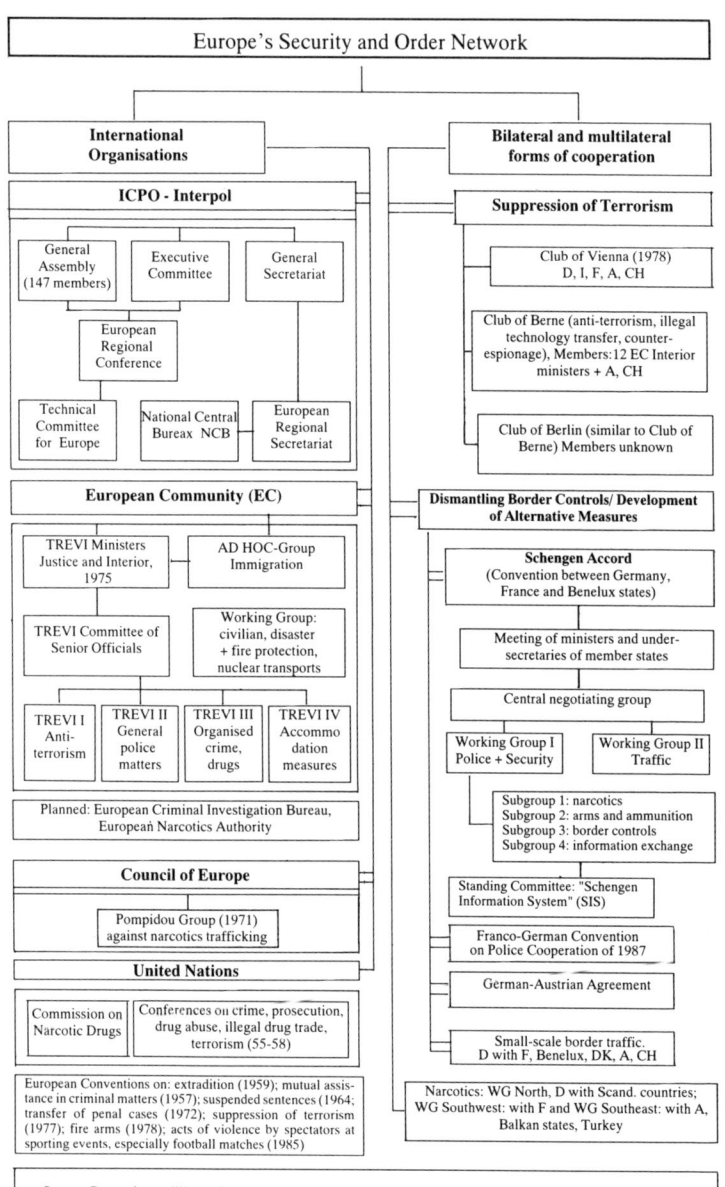

Source: Bürger kontrollieren die Polizei (Bremen), CILIP - Bürgerrechte + Polizei, Straßenmedizin (May 1990)

8. Reversion to Pre-democratic Conditions or Democratization of the EC's Politics and Economy?

Thesis 15

All the consequences and dangers of the Single Market that we have examined have shown a serious political and democratic deficiency. The market shapes reality to the advantage of capital, and politics not only lags behind it but also lacks instruments which are taken for granted at national level. Two key problems emerge: the European Parliament's lack of legislative power, and the lack of opportunities for direct involvement by the groups affected in local situations, above all the disadvantaged and their self-help and solidarity organizations. We should therefore demand the reform of the European Parliament, rights of involvement in decision-making for social movements and organizations, and a new, democratic communication structure.

In the lack of political controls over the economy, in the plutocratic relationship with the two-thirds world, in the Single Market's effect on the regions, the agricultural and social areas, ecology and finally the security situation – evident in all these is the absence of viable democratic politics. The Single Market for the economy runs on ahead; politics, and the people hurt by it, lag far behind.

After Kleinert, the former press spokesman for the Baden-Württemberg government under Prime Minister Späth, had moved to Daimler-Benz to be spokesman there, he was asked about his experience of the two sectors. His reply: "The economy makes reality, politics makes rhetoric."

This is a basic tendency in capitalism. But in the case of Europe it is made extremely sharp by the fact that so far the institutions make no provision for representative democracy. It is not an elected parliament that decides its laws but the Council of Ministers, which represents the governments of the member countries. The diagram that follows makes this clear.[58]

The schema shows the organs involved in the decision process and their composition. The European Council has not been considered here. In it the member states' heads of state and government have since 1975 been meeting twice a year to vote on basic Community problems and take fundamental political decisions, often on issues on which the Council of Ministers (as the EC's decision-making body) could reach no agreement. The European Council, for which there was originally no provision in the EC treaties, was formally included in the community constitution through Article 2 of the Single European Act (1986).

68   *Europe in the World System 1492 – 1992*

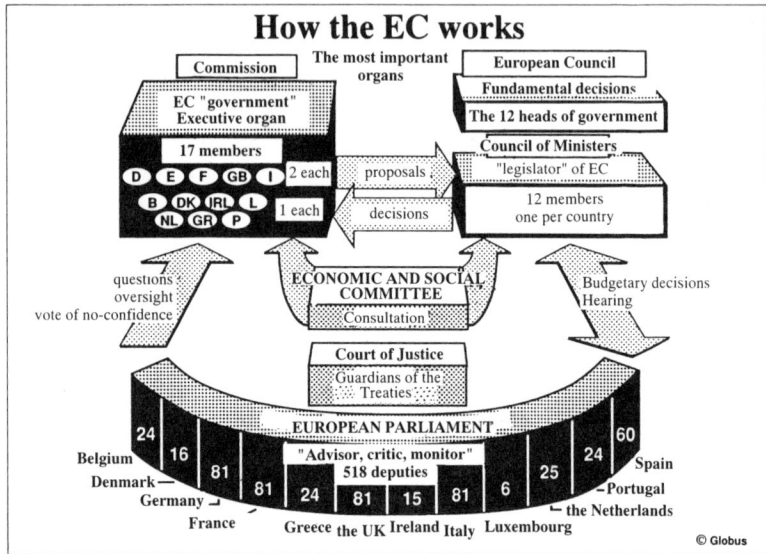

When we examine the particulars of the European Parliament's role, the following powers are distinguished:
• Helping with EC legislation. The diagram below shows how this works.[59]

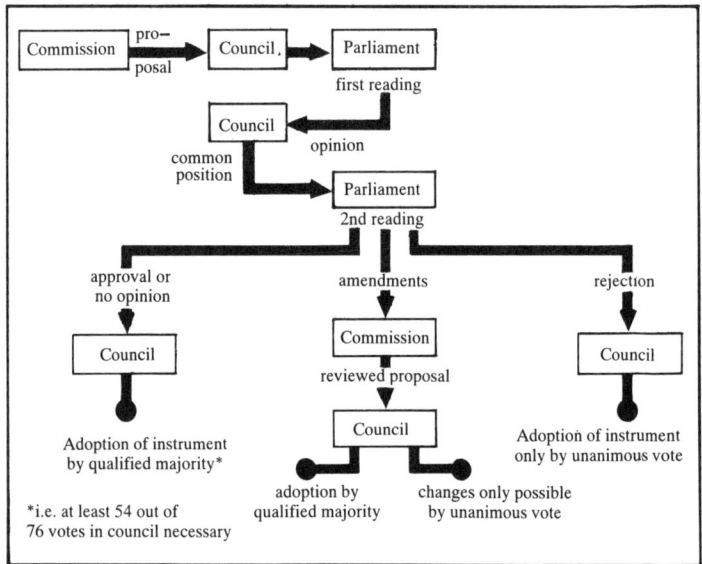

- Monitoring rights (parliamentary questions, actions before the European Court, votes of no-confidence in the Commission – all without real chances of success, but useful for clarifying issues).
- The right of budgetary control (a true power of decision only on the 30 percent of expenditure which is non-obligatory, just of alteration on the obligatory 70 percent).
- The right to consent to agreements on association and joining.

Real legislative power belongs to the Council of Ministers, thus to representatives of the national executives – against every rule of the classical democratic demand for power-sharing. Executive power is exercised by the Commission, which is likewise unelected by the Parliament. This cannot be tolerated in the future. For with the Single Market a tremendous amount of new power will pass to the European institutions, which will more and more take competences away from the governments – which are at least subject to representative democratic control, while they themselves have no democratic legitimation. That shows the vital importance of

Action goal 18:

The European Parliament must get all the powers that national parliaments in the Community have – and thus become the sovereign legislative body for the EC.[60]

But that is not enough. Laboriously, but also with relative success, movements and organizations of citizens with concerns in many aspects of justice, peace and the integrity of creation have tried to influence their local, regional and national political and social institutions in order at least to limit the destructive effects of the market on people and nature. With the Single European Market the economic and political decision-making processes will become yet more complex, and yet more distant from the people they touch. Transnational corporations are by their nature geared up to act and exchange information internationally, and they have the resources for it. Lest the people should be hopelessly outmanoeuvred, we must have two other action goals, and also work for the strengthening of the representative European Parliament:

Action goal 19:

New laws to give access to economic and political information and better public, civil control of the information and communication structures run by companies and banks.[61]

Action goal 20:

An effective guarantee of rights to be heard and to participate for self-help and solidarity groups of involved and, particularly, disadvantaged people, above all for minorities, who have no chance in the parliamentary, majority-rule system.

Now we come to the last part of our reflections: How can people in Europe respond to the morally ambiguous past, present and future of their continent? And what can they do about it?

Part III

Is Justice Possible?

1. Considerations of Strategy
2. Theological Considerations

1. Considerations of Strategy

Thesis 16

All the experience of history suggests that the existing political and economic institutions are unlikely of their own accord to renew themselves in such a way that the present tendency of the Western capitalist system to do more and more harm to people and damage to nature can be basically changed or even mitigated. On the other hand, the system's immense contradictions are generating an increasing readiness to resist, and alternatives and counter-strategies, in the civil society. Thus a double strategy recommends itself:

1) refusal to conform, and recourse to alternatives in small grassroots cells, with a view to the long-term transformation of the system;

2) the organization of countervailing power in coalitions of old and new social movements with a view to bringing short and medium term influence to bear on the system.

Both demand new methods of education and communication.

It goes against all experience of history, particularly during the last five hundred years of the Western capitalist system, to expect the political and economic institutions to be able of their own accord so to reform or transform themselves that the poor and nature will receive justice. It also goes against theological insights into the nature of human sin and its structural, supra-personal expression.

On the other hand there is also a history of resistance and the struggle for alternatives. I think of the struggle of Las Casas and many other religious with and after him for the aboriginal Americans' rights and alternative ways of life, of the slaves' self-liberation under Toussaint Louverture, of the struggle of the workers' movement since the nineteenth century, and of the popular struggles for liberation from colonialism. In this sense it is a sign of hope that, everywhere in the world, social, ecological and peace movements have come up and – even though they face pain and are often persecuted – are growing. They are often linked to base Christian communities. They are the new expression of a growing civil society, and have begun to make an impact on the economic and political institutions beyond that of the classical institutions of the labour movement.[1] They have interests in common because of the many contradictions that the capitalist accumulation model gives rise to, not just at the periphery and semi-periphery in the South but also in the regions of the centre.

Thus, when we were looking at the tendencies and possible effects of the Single European Market, we came across a number of self-help organizations of those it harms and movements in solidarity with them –

even if they are not yet fully developed and hardly linked up with each other: trade unions, initiatives for the unemployed, women's organizations, workers with migrants and refugees, alternative farmers, environment groups, non-governmental organizations to support the struggle of the two-thirds world. In North and South America movements of the indigenous Americans have, in view of the five hundred years of oppression and five hundred years of resistance, linked together and are laying down clear demands, above all for rights to their land, and the rewriting of their history from their own point of view and not that of the European and North American oppressors.

These movements of the people (of the civil society) are, despite the recent disappointments mentioned in the introduction, the point of departure for a liberation strategy. With the dangers to the environment in mind, and the militarism and re-arming which is spreading in spite of the end of the East-West conflict, there are interests that even transcend class differences. Karl Marx's assumption that only the industrial proletariat would bring about the changes to blow the system sky-high has been overtaken from three directions. Not only can the proletariat be co-opted; the "Lumpenproletariat" on the one hand and "partial victims" from the middle class on the other can be part of the transformation process.

Precisely this lies at the heart of most reactions by Latin American theologians, social scientists and grassroots workers to what has happened in Eastern Europe and the Soviet Union. Frei Betto sees popular organizations as the subject of the new participative culture.[2] Xabier Gorastiaga SJ, an economist from Nicaragua, speaks more broadly of an international, participative solidarity movement:

> We need to reinvent socialism in the context of a technical revolution, as part of an interconnected planet where alliances play a completely different role from that during the Cold War. We have to look for alliances between the South and the new movements in the North – the environmentalist movement, the women's movement, the pacifist movement and the liberation and emancipation of God's Word coming from the churches. We are presently living in one system, with one market that is dominated by capital from the "Group of 7" (G7). It is in the light of these powers that we must create what we call a third-world socialism, a criollo or native socialism. We need a socialism from the South, without dependence on European socialism, which in my experience was never authentic. There now exists a possibility for a new left in Latin America – democratic, popular and participatory, that destroys the totalitarian and vertical nature of the traditional left.[3]

The power of capital is organized transnationally. This is what makes it so difficult to control. The Communist Manifesto closed with the words: "Workers of the world unite!" But transnational capital can play the workers in the countries of the centre and the periphery off against each other. The big question for the future, therefore, is whether this can be avoided through the development and networking of new social movements. That will depend essentially on how widely insight spreads into the commonness of interests in view of the way everything fits together globally, i.e. into the fact that without a pooling of countervailing power the number of losers will get bigger and bigger and the number of winners smaller and smaller.

What, in concrete terms, could this building of countervailing power look like? I start from a *double strategy*:

1) rejecting the capitalist economy as far as possible and laying out alternatives in small cells (with a view to transforming it in the long term);

2) organizing in order to exercise pressure on the political-economic macrosystem (with a view to reforming it in the short term).

This is a starting-point similar to that proposed by Pascal de Pury in connection with a World Council of Churches study on alternative technologies.[4] On the one hand, ordinary people ("the people") must rediscover their ability to work and manage in alternative ways ("to master technologies"). Faced, on the other hand, with complex technological and politico-economic systems, they must learn to control those who rule these systems ("to master those who master the technological systems").

On 1: It would be naive to think that the transformation of our present world economic system could be brought about simply by the alternative life of separate, small cells. Yet this transformation will never be possible unless people at ground level experiment with alternatives and in this way rediscover their own power to determine, or at least help shape, their economic and political fate.

In Emmaus, Pennsylvania, is "Project Rebirth". About this Loren Halvorson tells the following story:[5]

> The town of Greenfield, Iowa, was in serious economic difficulty because of the depressive situation in farming in that area. The experts came and told the townspeople that they had 14 main problems. Enumerating everything that was going wrong for them gave them a feeling of powerlessness, as if they could do nothing for themselves. But they had heard of "Project Rebirth" and they invited a team from Emmaus to come to Greenfield. The Emmaus team went about things quite differently from their previous advisers. Instead of starting with the problems, "Project Rebirth" started with the possibilities. The people of Greenfield were asked to make a list of everything they could do themselves. They ended up with over one hundred items. They began to work on what they could do, and they discovered that they were actually working on what they had been told they couldn't do.

Halvorson closes with the observation that the economic problem was obviously a spiritual one. When the team from Emmaus touched the people's spirit by giving them hope, they began to develop initiatives and to act. The master of this art was Jesus in his work among ordinary people. He gave them confidence that God was among them and at work in them, and that brought healing, an upright step, independence from those who seemed powerful, and the beginning of a new life in community – even a willingness to suffer for truth and justice. "Your faith has made you whole." "The last will be first." Our renewal as human beings, the renewal of our culture, economy and politics, begins with the victims of economic, political and religious power.

In this sense initiatives to develop out of elements of the so-called informal economy alternative, decentralized economic units, whether in the form of elements of a subsistence economy, or producer-consumer cooperatives, or communes partly decoupled from the capitalist economy, are of great significance.[6] But it would grossly overburden these mostly small and weak grassroots initiatives if one were to expect from them the overthrow or the taming of the capitalist macro-system. However, they care for the soil from which alternatives grow and the spiritual springs of resistance and struggle with the macro-system.

On 2: In order to have an effect upon the macro-system its victims must organize. We in Germany have a historical problem to work on this. Our intellectuals tended to assume that it was enough to think and say what was reasonable, and those in power would hear and act. If they did not, the intellectuals would withdraw into the corner where those who knew better sulked. Here the ecology and peace movements have begun a change worth securing. Countervailing power arises only through organization.

But beware of any kind of "Messianism". All-or-nothing positions often lead to over-exertion and disappointment among activists. In view of the realities of power, the thing to do in each situation is to find and select, for concrete struggles, strategically important points from which to influence the politico-economic structures and institutions.

On the kind of countervailing power that comes from a new grassroots culture, it is important, moreover, to remember Martin Luther King's saying in the tradition of Gandhi: "The way is the goal." That is, the means by which the struggle is carried out should not betray the goal. It is not simply a matter of exchanging power elites. That was bureaucratic socialism's fatal illusion. The way to the political goal, struggling for socially and ecologically more responsible structures and institutions, already anticipates, even if in a symbolically broken manner, the development of a new quality of humanness and a new quality of relationship between human being and human being and humankind and nature. That too is why there is in this work and this struggle the joy of a new quality of life.

If these thoughts are right, short and mid-term political action and demands of the kind indicated in the action goals in Part II belong together with the strategy for fundamental, long-term change. Indeed, for the sake of actual people's lives and the earth itself, the two strategies must be linked.[7] That is why, in the not yet closed situation of Europe 1992, it is still worth making strenuous efforts to influence the institutions from below. If little can be expected from simple dialogue with them, it is vital to build the foundation group of a new society, which begins to live out alternatives from the bottom up and which brings grassroots pressure to bear on the institutions through dissent as well as concrete demands. It means that, as well as working as individuals and in small groups with long-term change in view, initiatives must be organized to enable us together to achieve short-term improvements. That can only be welcomed by those politicians in the official institutions who are themselves interested in social and ecological changes in the present politico-economic structures. For without pressure from below they are doomed to failure.

In this spirit Kairos Europa is planning a "people's parliament" in Strasbourg from 5 to 10 June 1992 as a crystallizing point for the promotion of a "justice network" involving marginalized groups and solidarity groups in Europe in cooperation with similar groups outside Europe.

> As preparations stand at present, the 750 or so representatives of self-help and solidarity groups from most of the countries of Europe and some regions of Africa, Asia and Latin America will meet in five commissions, which will work on the vision of an alternative Europe based on the satisfaction of basic needs. There will also be workshops, which will look at the interconnection of the different experiences of suffering in terms of root causes and strategy. Through a big demonstration and in round-table discussions with European parliamentarians these will then be taken to the public and the decision-making channels. In connection with this a youth delegation might go from Strasbourg to Brussels, to speak directly to the Commission. To coincide with this, actions are planned in several European cities in order to demonstrate the growing grassroots presence in European questions and to exercise pressure on the decision-making bodies.[8]

This is only one of many initiatives which are taking the symbolic year 1992 as an occasion for developing new alliances for justice.[9] There was a big meeting of Christian base communities on this theme in Paris in July 1991.[10] The Franciscans are calling a meeting of Christian base groups in Assisi, also in June 1992. BUKO (Federal Congress of World Development Groups) is planning actions and events at the next G7 world economic summit in Munich in July 1992. It is an event of almost historic significance that in Germany a "bridge forum" for cooperation between environment groups, trade unions and third-world organizations has been formed.[11] A common clearing-house is being set up for this. It provides a platform for developing further relations between old and new social movements, which have been tense so far. At the European level there are also regular coordination meetings of the various campaigns. In the USA "Kairos North America" has been formed. In Latin America there are a large number of initiatives, by the Latin American Council of Churches amongst others. International networking has begun in many alliances, large and small.

All this appears very inadequate, faced as we are with the concentrations of power in the Western/European politico-economic system. But

David overcame Goliath in spite of Goliath's mighty arms and strength. The temple on which David hit him with his stone is in our case the system's inability to control people completely. As long as people, faced with the contradictions which capitalism necessarily creates, are able to feel pain, the system will never be in complete control. It certainly tries to anaesthetize people and lead them astray by changing information into entertainment and disinformation, and life into consumption, but that can never be completely successful. The American military secret service is right to be afraid of popular movements, base communities, liberation theologians, solidarity groups and churches that work with the poor. For though military, political and economic power is in safe hands, the "hearts and minds" of people are not. This is our "capital".

But this "capital", people who swim against the tide, can only be increased if counter-strategies in education and communication are developed as well. The base communities and popular movements in Brazil and in other parts of Latin America were possible only because of Paulo Freire's "pedagogy of the oppressed", which makes people, by analyzing their own social situation and discovering their own potential, subjects of their own history – as the people of Greenfield also found. What we in Europe need is a training programme for "multipliers" from grassroots groups, like that which CESEP in Sao Paulo provides for Latin America. All over Latin America information and documentation centres are growing, which systematically counteract the disinformation churned out by those in economic, political and military power. In our part of the world too, a similar culture of alternative education and critical counter-information emerged long ago. At the European level, networking between alternative information groups and institutions has started.[12] It is worth strengthening this development.

Is there a way of justice in Europe after five hundred years of looting, oppression and the making and worship of money? Despite all the signs of hope I have mentioned, we are seized by deep doubts. If we had to base our capacity for action exclusively on a rational calculation of our chance of success, we would probably prefer to give up now rather than later. The realistic chances of being able to give a positive answer to our question are, after the rather paralyzing historical experiences of the period we have considered, not very high. But are there other perspectives? An approach which might enlarge on the purely economic and political is that of theology.

2. Theological Considerations

How can we as Europeans deal theologically with 500 years of looting, oppression and the making and worship of money?

> The kairos, as the Bible understands it, is the time when the night is gone, the time for us to wake from sleep (Rom.13:11-14). The kairos compels us to

become prophets of justice for ourselves and our fellow human beings, it compels us to overcome fear and to fight. But the kairos is the moment of hope. The kairos is the beginning of the day, in whose light we are able to take steps together in liberation. The kairos demands decisions of us as individuals, but also much harder decisions of our church institutionsl.[13]

Thesis 17

A possible category from biblical theology for confronting the Western world system's history and present, seen from the perspective of its human victims and nature, is that of the "kingdoms of this world". Their power, the Bible says, is judged and broken already. The kingdom of God is their opposite and, in the victory of the crucified Messiah, it vindicates the poor and the oppressed. Seen in these terms, could 1992 be the time of decision (kairos) for Europe – the time of judgment and the time for a new beginning? Christian base communities could contribute to the social movements' struggle out of a hope which does not depend on success. Europe's mainstream churches face the question of whether they are prepared to break with traditional theologies legitimizing the economy, the state and the institutional church and become prophetic churches. That involves re-evaluating Western forms of democracy and freedom; in concrete terms it means denouncing the world economy's plutocracy and its murderous security system, and making a critically constructive intervention to improve real democracy in the West – particularly in the fluid situation of the Single European Market. But a statement of repentance by the churches would be serious only if it had consequences (1) in the structures of the churches themselves, and (2) in their clear support for the victims' own organizations. The "righteousness of God through faith" would come about in close touch with them and lead to practical justice.

When I look at the five-hundred-year history of the world system which Western Europe has shaped, I cannot help thinking of the category in biblical theology of "the kingdoms of this world". The attempt at a Spanish empire, the Pax Britannica, the Pax Americana and its twin sister the Pax Sovietica, and the three-headed "beast from the abyss" (cf. Rev.13) which has now emerged, are as "conformed to this world" (Rom.12:2) as the Persian empire, in which the first apocalyptic writings and visions of the fall of empires and the coming of the "human" kingdom of God emerged (Dan.7). Historically, moreover, the Western system is in many ways heir to the Roman empire, against which the apocalypse of John (Revelation) preaches its message of hope about the fall of the "whore of Babylon" and all who became rich through her (ch.18).[14] Of it Jesus says that his kingdom is not of the same kind, and that he does not give peace (pax) as the Roman world system does, namely by subjugation and force.[15]

The heart of the question for this biblical tradition is: Who is king? In today's speech, who has power? This is the basic theme of the dialogue between Jesus and Pilate, the bearer of Roman power, the emperor's surrogate in Palestine; it is also what precipitates Jesus' crucifixion (John 19).[16] Pilate states that he has the power of life and death over Jesus – over the whole of humanity (v.10). But Jesus answers: "You would have no power over me unless it had been given to you from above" (v.11). That means it is not power in itself that is evil. All power is from God and therefore good. But it is sin, offence against the first commandment, to think, act or set up political and economic structures as if the fullness of power belonged to oneself. For that reason it is wrong to treat questions of the economy and politics primarily or exclusively as ethical questions. First and foremost they are theo-logical questions. In the Great Catechism Luther correctly treats them primarily as questions about the first commandment.[17] The question "Who is king?" means the same as the question "Who is God?" So the Jews say to Pilate: "We have no king but Caesar" (v.15). They had forgotten that in their scriptures there is already the report of a dispute like this. When Israel wants to have a king "like the other peoples", God says to Samuel: "They have not rejected you, but they have rejected me from being king over them" (1 Sam. 8:7). "The kingdom of God", the central point of Jesus' teaching, means "the enthronement of God" (*malkuth Jahweh*). Jesus is the "Son of Man" with whom the kingdom of God comes (Dan.7) – people living together with God and with each other and with nature in a community with a human face (as opposed to kingdoms that are embodied as wild, voracious beasts).

Jesus does not fight for power in these world systems; he and his "kingdom" embody the opposition, the alternatives to these systems. He is the Messiah, i.e. the anointed "king" in God's kingdom. And this king lets the crown of thorns be stuck on his head, he lets the purple robe of scorn be put on him, he lets himself be tortured. He witnesses to the truth, the faithfulness and the justice of God. He shows the traits of the Suffering Servant from the prophecy of Isaiah 53. "Here is the man!" says Pilate. And this man, who does not recognize the power of the system, is so threatening to this power that it punishes him with the punishment for political revolutionaries, the cross.

Thus the US-trained and US-financed military of El Salvador had to shoot Archbishop Romero when he called upon soldiers to disobey orders, and kill the liberation theologians around Ellacuria, because they helped overcome fear of and dependence on the system in people's "hearts and minds" (he had been branded as a Marxist enemy in secret papers accepted also by the US army chief).[18]

Now, a counter-argument is often adduced against using Jewish and New Testament apocalyptic to explain the present situation: Is it not a demonizing of the economic and political structures that deters one from doing anything concrete about them? This misunderstanding is possible only if one does not realize the apocalyptic writings are resistance literature from the underground.[19] "Apokalypsis", revelation, is not concerned with presenting terrible events, as commonly understood. Rather, the seer sees and proclaims to the persecuted and the suffering that in God the powers, which lay claim here to absolute power, are already judged and disempowered, that Christ, the gentle Lamb, has the victory, and with him those who endure to the end in resistance and do not bow before the whore of Babylon and her merchants.

For those disadvantaged and persecuted by the system, for those who bear witness to their crucified Messiah in resistance for truth and faithfulness, there is no greater, firmer, more unshakeable consolation, no surer hope, than believing the revelation that the powers are already judged, that they stand on feet of clay, and that the peacemakers and those who hunger and thirst for justice will be victors with the crucified Messiah, that God is already preparing the new earth and the new heaven. Those who think they can do without this perspective, the conviction that God himself executes the judgment on Pharaoh, Babylon, Rome, Western Europe, the USA and Japan – and the accumulators of capital – and builds the new earth among and with the oppressed and persecuted, go without the last ground of hope, and may therefore be tempted either to displace reality in its nastiness or give way to despair.

Augustine, the church father, made – learning from apocalyptic and the North African, Tychonius – a fundamental criticism of imperialism on the model of Rome. He unmasked the Roman principle of *parcere subiectis et debellare superbos* (protect the subdued and subdue the proud by war) as power putting itself in God's place, depending on the basic perversion of substituting love of self for the love of God and man. He found this struggle between two ways of life, groups of people and tendencies within one person (with God in love and against God in self-love) in the whole of history since creation. We can learn from Augustine that a critique of imperialism must always be a critique of all relationships – from the way individuals conduct their lives to the politico-economic macro-structures and, indeed, the whole cosmos. That means it is always a matter of changing structures and persons at the same time.[20]

Augustine wrote his book *De Civitate Dei* after the fall of Rome in 410 AD, after the western Goths under Alaric had conquered and destroyed the city. That was in some ways easy in comparison with our task.

For the beast whose blood is money (Hobbes), the world system under which two-thirds of humankind suffer and which quite openly gives egoism as its basic principle, is now attempting a new triumph. It has forced down another empire by a terrible arms race and has just subdued a proud opponent by war; now it seems to stand alone as the undisputed victor. The whole world bows before it. Anyone who does not is either taken for a fool or eliminated.

In this situation it is of inestimable significance to gain from the biblical message the clear view and confidence that this power is already judged, that its feet are crumbling, its inner contradictions pointing to an incurable illness, and that the signs of God's kingdom and salvation are growing, hidden, among us. This orientation to the nearness of God's judgment and his saving acts, revealed in God's Messiah, is marked in the New Testament by the Greek expression "kairos". It means the moment of decision which one may not pass by, but also the God-given chance to seize it – to turn from love of self in dependence on the powers of death to free life by the love of God in justice.

This is the perspective and the basis not only of the historic peace churches (Mennonites, Brethren, Quakers, etc.) but also of countless Christian base communities all over the world. In form they range from classical orders to grassroots groups, so in no way do they all have the same intensity, quality and radiance. Therefore we must not idealize them. But I believe that they have a special contribution to make in the struggle of the victims and their social movements.[21]

1. Christian base communities are able to ground themselves securely in unshakeable hope in the kingdom of God, which is already among us, as Jesus said. Thus their hope reaches far beyond the results of what they do, beyond disappointments, their own weaknesses and even beyond death. The expression of this hope is their prayer, their secure foundation in the biblical message that God himself vindicates the poor, their sharing of the bread of life and the wine of salvation and liberation, their fellowship in and with Jesus the Messiah and with the poor. "The kingdom of God does not mean food and drink but justice and peace and joy in the Holy Spirit" (Rom.14:17). In all the exertion of the struggle this hope in the Holy Spirit gives breath, deep breath and joy.

They are – in their being, not primarily in what they do – a sign of God's loving creativity, of the power of God's Spirit to change people from I-centred individuals into people in a new fellowship with God and with each other. There are, of course, conflicts and crises even in base communities. But they are proof that crises and conflicts can be solved in ways other than those of oppression and force. So they are the salt of the earth and the light of the world. In view particularly of how disappointing most of the institutional churches are, they are for many Christians a source of hope – hope that God is stronger than our sin and mortality.

2. Christian base communities and groups need take no account of dependence on money. They can thus name the name and expose the destructive character of the power of capital, which claims power of decision over the life and death of people and nature. In this way they can break through the taboo that surrounds – as if they were gods – the mechanisms of capital growth and fight for space. Thus they can refuse to honour the "emperor" of this realm as once the Christians in Rome did –

which, in the two-thirds world, the periphery of the imperium, can admittedly lead to martyrdom. We should not underestimate the power given to base communities in this respect. For five hundred years the core of the capitalist system has been the progressive capitalization of the world for the sake of more and more power and wealth. So it touches a nerve when a member of a community in Ireland, Dara Molloy, says: "We are trying to marginalize money." Pushing back as far as possible the power of apparently all-ruling money in our society in Europe is perhaps the most important task of the base communities. This is about no more and no less than disempowering the death-idol Mammon and creating space for the God of love and justice. At this point the base communities touch and influence the root of all the spiritual and all the social and ecological problems of our Western society. In this they set up signs of orientation and hope for all people, not just Christians.

3. At a time when there seem to be no alternatives, Christian base communities can live an alternative – including owning goods in common, running their own economies on ecological lines, developing new relationships between men and women and truly democratic forms of decision-making. The weakness of bureaucratic socialism, that of seeking new social structures without renewing people, is overcome in a base community. Thus they are the salt of a new culture and light for others who seek a way of justice between the darkness and the deceiving spotlights of the world system.

More than anything else we need examples that are possible as alternatives. Of course we cannot argue, either from the biblical promise or a realistic analysis, that all people should be organized in base communities. That will happen only when the kingdom of God comes in its fullness. But the signs we have are a source of hope.

The way of justice attempted by Christian base communities, which only those without understanding misinterpret as a flight from the world, is highly political, since it rejects the basic principle of the kingdoms of this world and lives out a fundamental alternative – like the Messiah, Jesus of Nazareth, who neatly sums up his politico-economic analysis and counter-plan in these words:

> You know that those who are supposed to rule over the Gentiles lord it over them, and their great men do violence to them. But it shall not be so among you; but whoever would be great among you must be your servant, and whoever would be first among you must be the slave of all. For the Son of Man also came not to be served but to serve, and to give his life as a ransom for many. (Mark 10:42-45).

This raises for the question of the kairos, the time of decision for and in Europe, a problem that goes back in history even farther than five hundred years. It concerns the relationship of the mainstream churches to state and power since the so-called Constantinian change. In 312 AD the

Roman emperor Constantine gave up the persecution of Christians and himself became a Christian; a few decades later Emperor Theodosius proclaimed Christianity the state religion. Did this not take away the social-historical basis of the primitive Christian, apocalyptic attitude to state and power? Did not the church *have* to find a new approach to a state and a society that declared itself in principle open to the Christian message? Would it not have been a betrayal of God's love of justice, peace and his creation not to have taken such responsibility?[22]

The South African Karios Document tries to deal with this problem by distinguishing between "state theology, church theology and prophetic theology", and Luise and Willy Schottroff have presented the biblical traditions and ways of interpreting them which stand behind these types of theology.[23]

State theology seeks its biblical foundation in those texts in which the young Israelite kingdom under Saul, David and Solomon in the tenth century BC strives to prevail against the resistance of the free peasants in particular (cf. Judg. 9).

Ancient oriental kingship ideology, according to which the king as son of god takes care of external security and peace and internal law, justice and welfare, is used for this (cf. e.g. Ps. 71). In an impressive monograph entitled *Ma'at. Justice and Immortality in Ancient Egypt*, Jan Assmann has worked out the origin and structure of this complex of ideas. In our terms the important point is that, in the situation of an emerging class society, the king is the guarantor of justice, that he protects the poor and the weak from the power of the wealthy (big landowners, officials, etc.). Assmann calls this the principle of "vertical solidarity" (*Ma'at*, justice from above). When Israel had introduced kingship, this was obviously the point at which Jahweh's will on the Law could be linked to traditional concepts, even though it really implies a non-hierarchical social structure (called by Assmann the model of "horizontal solidarity"). There are two kings, David for the whole kingdom and Josiah for the Southern kingdom, which, according to the witness of the biblical traditions comes close to the ideal of just kingship. Deuteronomy gave the classical picture of a king who would be acceptable to Jahweh and consistent with Israel's intended alternative society: he should be from the people and should not set himself above the people, he should not heap up privileges and should follow closely the law of Jahweh (Deut. 17:14-20). I call this the "power-taming" model. But the bottom line is Israel's kingship experiment failed (in 722 finally for the Northern kingdom and in 586 for the Southern kingdom). Instead of creating rights for the poor and the weak against the rich and the strong, the kings were mostly an expression of a society in the process of division.

From the ninth century, the time of Elijah and Elisha, the prophets therefore made alliances with the free peasants, the poor and the oppressed, against the crown, in order to stand firmly for the kingdom of God and God's justice against power. Amos, Isaiah and Micah are the best-known names. That is why the Kairos Document gives to this critical initiative the name of *prophetic theology*.

However, state theology takes care to bring one New Testament text above all into the field: Paul's Letter to the Romans, thirteenth chapter, verses 1-7. This says, among other things: "Let everyone be subject to those raised to (public) power. For there is no (public) power except from God ... For those in (public) power are not a terror to good conduct, but to bad ... "[24]

Luise Schottroff has shown that this passage belongs to the tradition of Jewish and Christian texts which try to come to terms with the situation of the people of God under the rule of world empires after the destruction of the independent state in 586 BC.

What is crucial is that the people keep their covenanted freedom to live according to the Torah, according to the will of God. As long as that is possible, they can offer a degree of loyalty to the imperial power (Jeremiah, Daniel, Jesus in Mark 12:13-17). The further point is made in Romans 13 that the community can also recognize that, if in the Roman empire evil is punished by public law, good is rewarded – and God wants what is good. On this point, therefore, a declaration of loyalty can be given. But this is less than what the empire wants. It wants total recognition, it demands sacrifice to the emperor. So despite declarations of relative loyalty, as in Romans 13, Christians were persecuted, even as Jesus was crucified despite his saying that Pilate's power was given to him by God. Therefore chapter 13 of the Revelation of John, in which the same Roman empire is presented as the beast from the abyss, does not contradict Romans 13. The tension between the two texts expresses the fact that a community, which practises only a relative form of loyalty to the empire – and thus has no direct political overthrow in mind, but rejects the empire's structures through their "No" to absolute obedience and their alternative life – is in unending conflict with the system and in an extreme case will suffer martyrdom.

State theology may not be based on Romans 13:1-7, then; and indeed, no direct ethical directives may be drawn from it in the event Christians themselves take up political power. There is not a single text about that in the whole New Testament, for it lay outside the concrete socio-political conditions of primitive Christianity. What should we do, then, if this situation occurs?

First we must establish that it is a legitimate question. Each new historical situation must be judged by the spirit of the biblical tradition, not by its letter. The Bible itself reflects a constant struggle to assess anew with God each historical challenge out of the experience of the faith so far. And there is just such a turning-point in the Hebrew Bible, when Israel, later divided into the Northern and Southern kingdoms, had between the sixteenth and eleventh centuries BC to grapple with the fact that it was a kingdom like any other. At that time there was an attempt – then unsuccessful – to bind the politico-economic structures of the kingdom to the Law of Jahweh in order to tame power. Inasmuch as Western churches (and theologians) after Constantine have tried to bind power to the law and at the same time maintain a prophetic, critically constructive distance from that power, they can relate to a particular, if also unsuccessful, phase of the history of Israel. Has this approach stood the test in Western history, and is it still a legitimate option in view of Europe's present situation? This question and possible answers to it need intensive further work and can only be dealt with briefly here.

There is law and law. The Law of ancient Israel seeks, in a situation of asymmetrical power between the parties to a conflict, to protect and support the weaker in accordance with Jahweh's loving, saving dealings. The Hebrew word for "to judge", *saphat*, means to restore a troubled relationship. Thus "judge" means "saviour" – for the poor and weak.[25] So in the biblical sense justice must always be seen "from below", from the point of view of the weaker party. Roman law is for the protection of property and its owners. Overlooking that led Luther to his fatal misunderstanding, and the mistaken action in the Peasants' War. Despite all his theologically important reflection on the reform of imperial law on the Roman model, its effect was to support rising absolutism.[26]

But there is one problem we must work on in a completely new way, above all because of today's situation and with Europe's five-hundred-year old history in the world system in mind. It is a problem fraught with ambiguities which cloud the church's ability to make theological judgments. It is the problem of *democracy* and, in its train, that of *freedom*. Here the Western churches seem to have it easy. For is not the democratic state with its law and constitution by definition bound to the law, and therefore in the tradition of the "taming of power" which has always been theologically legitimate?

At this point we ought to investigate the history of law and constitutions in capitalist Western states. Certainly, there are achievements here that are worth defending, that can be affirmed in order to extend and develop them further. Among them, surely, are the control of political power by the sharing of powers, and human rights – particularly if individual citizens' rights are supplemented by social and ecological rights, as is being attempted through the UNO. But there have been and there are deficiencies, increasingly big ones even, in the Western form of democracy, which are scarcely noticed even in very respectable attempts to penetrate the question of democracy theologically.[27]

Since John Locke, the father of Western constitutions, the protection of property has been seen as the bourgeois state's main task.[28] Property is defined as not only what one owns in goods and means of production but

Is Justice Possible? 87

also one's own person, particularly one's own labour, and one's personal rights. But no-one asks which owner has greater power in the socio-economic struggle, the owner of labour or the owner of the means of production. In this way the state in the end protects the stronger (namely the owners of capital) unless the weaker fight for their rights. And this tendency is still evident, even after slavery – looking suspiciously like a mutation of Western democracy – has been abolished.

The problem has become sharper in the last twenty years, as capital has made itself transnational and thus withdrawn even more from democratic control by political institutions. In the EC there is the further problem that the market has established itself without a representative parliament exercising legislative powers and the possibility of an effective social policy. In the recent phase of development, moreover, capital has, as I have said, succeeded in winning the state over for the interests of the concentration and accumulation of capital and in steadily dismantling the rights fought for by the labour movements, even in the centre countries.

As we have seen, internationally our governments are not only keen to support wholly undemocratic or quasi-democratic governments as long as they leave Western capital a free hand, they also take full responsibility together, in the world economic summit of the seven big industrialized nations (G7), for the plutocracy of the world economic institutions which exercise almost dictatorial power over the debtor countries of the two-thirds world. Low Intensity and Mid-Intensity security strategies are the means of preventing social movements for a more just and democratic social order from developing. Over and above that, the Santa Fe II document shows, as I have pointed out, that the idea of democracy itself is, right from its liberal origins, bound to property. What is given as the *social content of democracy*, therefore, is the *free capital market* and *free enterprise*. Among the political institutions, elected governments are reckoned to be "temporary governments". More important are the "permanent forms of government" of the military, the civil service, and the judiciary and police, the document says – and calls all this "democratic capitalism".

This shows that the idea of *freedom* too which, along with that of democracy, stamps Western ideology, is marked by the same ambiguity. In the liberal world market freedom means the power of the stronger, as far as enslaving through debt people they have subjugated for five hundred years in countries they made dependent on them. And where the freedom of weaker groups in the centre countries is relatively protected by the state social policy and by the countervailing power of the trade unions and the new social movements, the transnational power of capital increasingly undermines these rights. So one can never take "democracy" and "freedom" as purely political themes, but must always see them in their politico-economic context.

In this situation the kind of theology which the South African Kairos Document calls *church theology* is particularly dangerous. By "reconciliation" it means "compromise" with the powerful. In an asymmetrical power situation that means taking sides with the stronger party. Reconciliation without justice and restitution is the continuation of injustice. It overlooks the fact that in the New Testament, loving one's enemies means bringing them through prayer, love and open confession of the truth to repentance, to change in the sense of a new community.[29]

What are the consequences of all this for the mainstream churches in the light of five hundred years of history and Europe's new concentration of power?

• If one looks at the atrocities committed in this period in the name of Christ and the church, one could speak of negative evidence about God. The image of Christ was in many cases completely obscured, even turned into its opposite, beginning with what Las Casas described of the many examples of conscious or unconscious identification and coalition between mission and colonialism, right up to the German Christians' support of Hitler, and Bush's blasphemous prayers at the time of the Gulf war. The year 1992 is the year in which we and our churches, if we still want to be worthy of the name of Christians and churches of Christ, have a chance publicly and unambiguously to break with every kind of power-conforming "state theology" and camouflaging "church theology". The idea and practice of Western democracy are also under test. The criterion is the question of where in our national and European constitutions and institutions, and equally in the international constitutions of the United Nations, law in the biblical sense of law for the weak is or is not protected. Where it is not, we must intervene prophetically for law for the weak, not law for the majority, and demand new democratic structures to secure it – particularly in a situation that is still partly open like that, at present, in Western Europe.

• With regard to the structures of the world economy, we have given in, openly and in the name of democracy and freedom, to the dictatorship of transnational capital and its maintenance by murderous strategies of conflict. The mainstream churches have not noticed that in these five hundred years the isssue of power that demands absolute obedience has shifted from the arena of politics to that of economics. Therefore we as Christians and churches, faced with the cries of the victims of five hundred years of exploitation and genocide, must fundamentally reject not just state theology and church theology but also every theology that accommodates itself to the laws of capitalist economics. *Economic theology* is about sacrificing to Caesar under today's conditions. It is not about the market as an instrument for supplying and distributing goods people produce, in order to satisfy basic human needs. We would have to say "yes" to that, as Romans 13 did to the legal function of the Roman empire. But we are called

Is Justice Possible? 89

to say "no" to the capitalist, so-called free market, which is geared to the accumulation of more and more power and wealth by a few and which today offers itself as a "total market".

How might Europe's mainstream churches make this prophetic renunciation of economic, state and church theology? From the theological point of view, a confession of repentance might take the form of what Dietrich Bonhoeffer proposed which – although composed in the specific context of the Nazi dictatorship and its persecution of the Jews – expresses the essentials of the whole five-hundred year epoch:

> The church confesses that it has seen the arbitrary use of brutal violence, the physical and mental suffering of countless innocent people, oppression, hatred and murder, without raising its voice for them, without having found ways to come to their help. It has become guilty of the lives of the weakest and most defenceless of the brothers of Jesus Christ.[30]

If, however, one considers the feeble way in which the German churches themselves went about the Stuttgart Confession,[31] and how the formulations from the ecumenical assemblies of the conciliar process for "Justice, Peace and the Integrity of Creation" are in danger of serving purely rhetorical ends, one hesitates about working on a statement of repentance for the churches.

If the churches generally are aware of the spiritual duty and the opportunity to take a step of repentance in 1992 – and few signs of this are visible in the public faces of congregations and mainstream churches – it can be worth taking seriously only if its clear consequences in terms of the double strategy become reflected in their own (structural) being and action. That should then comprise the following elements:

1. The churches can take part in long-term transformation strategies:

• by refusing to give legitimation to the neo-liberal capitalist system at precisely the moment when this presents itself as one without alternatives and further suppresses social and ecological needs;

• by detaching themselves institutionally, as far as possible, from the capitalist money economy and the class society (e.g. through alternative investments and their own church terms of employment, which at least reduce the salary differentials between different classes of staff and introduce highest and lowest income norms);

• by giving open support to the organizations of those, outside and within Europe, who suffer under the West European system, and the movement in solidarity with them, in their efforts to develop alternatives. That would mean the churches' working hand-in-hand with those who, as the biblical message says, are first in the kingdom of God, and thus taking part themselves – perhaps as the last – in this kingdom of love.

2. The churches can share in strategies of short-term reform by taking part in coalitions which exercise organized pressure for social and ecologi-

cal improvement on the politico-economic macro-systems. Their partners in coalition would be:
- organizations of the disadvantaged;
- old and new social and ecological movements;
- minorities in the political and economic institutions, who work within them for social and ecological improvement (in Europe, for example, a not inconsiderable number of members of the European Parliament and the Council of Europe).

In this way the churches would take on their prophetic task, which consists of uncovering and naming injustice in the power structures and getting involved in order to influence macro-systems according to God's will, i.e. for the good of God's creation and people.

Such sharing in strategies of transformation and of reform assume a profound conversion on the part of Christians, congregations and churches. The Kairos Documents from South Africa and Central America and the Damascus Document produced by a team of theologians from the two-thirds world[32] have called us to just such a repentance and conversion. We know we can meet the challenge such conversion involves neither as individuals nor as churches. How could we meet it, how could we make restitution for the guilt that we have loaded on ourselves through five hundred years of exploitation and genocide? And how could we shake off all at once the "structures of sin" that have grown throughout history or change them to structures of justice and restitution, which is what our conversion must involve if it is to mean anything?

Our situation is a tangible example of what classical theology called original sin. So we are fearful, and we see no way out. For us who are unjust, justice can start only when the victims of our injustice take the initiative and accept us. That happens when they ask us, their enemies, to become their friends and to take their side in their struggle for justice. In Matthew's Gospel (25:31ff.) we read that Jesus is hidden in those who are hungry, thirsty, naked, homeless and deprived of liberty. We hear that mostly as a challenge. But it also says that we *can* meet God in the poor, if we act in solidarity with those whose basic needs are denied by the system. The poor are Christ in the present, in whom forgiveness is offered to us as we are invited to take, without preconditions, their side and thus God's side. Without the invitation of those who are oppressed by us, without our acceptance of their invitation to walk hand-in-hand with them, we cannot experience the joy of liberation.

The film *The Mission* about the Jesuits in Paraguay includes an impressive scene. A Spanish slave-trader is convinced by one of the Jesuits that he can be released from his guilt if he carries his fire-arms to the Indios and asks for forgiveness. The film shows how the man hauls the heavy burden up the mountain and falls down before the Indios. For a moment they take up the fire-arms in order to shoot the hated enemy. Then one of them cuts the rope. The bundle of fire-arms falls down the mountain, the enemies are able to embrace each other, and from then on the "converted" Spaniard lives and fights on their side.

In the same way the Kairos Documents are one of the signs that God accepts us in our victims – in him who was crucified by us, and his poor – and that with one cut of his knife he will free us from the guilt and burden of the past if we are prepared to be embraced by them and to join their side in the fight to win other enemies over as friends. In classical theology that means accepting "the righteousness of God through faith" (Rom.3:21ff.). It leads to the forging of the "weapons of injustice" into "weapons of justice" (Rom. 6:13). It also leads to non-conformity with the "structures of this world" (*schemata tou kosmou*) and to discerning and doing the will of God – "what is good and acceptable and perfect" (Rom. 12:2).

Notes

Introduction
[1] Beaud, p.12.
[2] See Duchrow, 1991, and de Santa Ana *et al.*, 1990.
[3] Cf. CCPD/WCC, 1991, p.11ff.
[4] Cf. Duchrow/Eisenbürger/Hippler.

Part I
[1] For more about the method for this see section 5 below.
[2] Transl. from Gutiérrez, p.141.
[3] Las Casas, p.13.
[4] Transl. from Gutiérrez, p.197; cf. Las Casas, p.26.
[5] *Ibid.*, p.127.
[6] Kennedy, p.64.
[7] Besides Mires, see Galeano, his classic book on the history of Latin America suffering from the Western invasion.
[8] Mires, p.13.
[9] Bauer, pp.112ff.
[10] Cf. Zinn, p.62.
[11] See Armstrong.
[12] Cf. Mires, pp.17ff.
[13] *Ibid.*, p.15.
[14] Las Casas, pp.85f. Cf. Luther on the banking and trading companies and their monopolistic practices: "... They have all wares under their control and they do with them as they want and without any hesitation. They produce those things so that (the prices) rise or fall as they please, and press and ruin all small traders, just like pike with the small fish in the water, as if they were lords over God's creatures and free from all laws of faith and love" (*Of Trade and Usury*, 1524).
[15] Aristotle, *Politikoon* ("On Politics"), book I, ch. 8-13.
[16] Wallerstein, pp.21ff.
[17] See *ibid.*, pp.24ff., 82ff. and Zinn, p.10.
[18] Cf. *ibid.*, p.86.
[19] Cf. *ibid.*, p.108ff.
[20] Cf. Wallerstein.
[21] See Zinn, pp.55 and 226ff.
[22] *Ibid.*, pp.24ff and 55ff.
[23] Kennedy, p.5.

[24] *Ibid.*, p.7.
[25] Zinn, pp.150ff.
[26] *Ibid.*, pp.170ff, 201ff.
[27] *Ibid.*, p.176.
[28] *Ibid.*, pp.245ff.
[29] *Ibid.*, pp.249ff.
[30] *Ibid.*, p.252.
[31] Cf. Duchrow, 1987, p.117, quoting from an unpublished paper by Galtung. See also Gross.
[32] Todorov.
[33] Mires, p.36.
[34] Cf. *ibid.*, p.42.
[35] *Ibid.*, pp.82ff.
[36] *Ibid.,* pp.51ff.
[37] On the following cf. Mires, pp.67ff.
[38] *Ibid.*, p.71.
[39] Cited from Mires, p.74.
[40] Cf. *ibid.*, p.77.
[41] Cf. *ibid.*, pp.101ff., 125ff.
[42] Cf. *ibid.*, pp.210ff.
[43] Cf. *ibid.*, pp.120ff., 147ff.; also Gutiérrez.
[44] On this event cf. Gutiérrez, pp.166ff.
[45] Cf. Duchrow, 1987, pp.36ff., 53ff., and 176.
[46] Cf. e.g. Zinn, p.267, and Wallerstein, pp.32ff.
[47] Kennedy, p.69ff.
[48] Cf. *ibid.*, p.103; Mires, pp.12ff.; Wallerstein, pp.191ff.
[49] Wallerstein, p.352.
[50] Cf. Lüthi.
[51] Wallerstein, p.38.
[52] On the following see Wallerstein, pp.199ff.; Kennedy, pp.85ff., and Beaud, pp.25ff.
[53] See Kennedy, pp.101ff., and Wallerstein, pp.273ff.
[54] Cf. Kennedy, pp.78ff., Beaud, pp.27ff., and in more detail Hill, 1961 and 1969.
[55] Wallerstein, pp.228ff.
[56] *Ibid.*
[57] *Ibid.*, pp.231ff.
[58] Meueler, pp.30f.
[59] Williams, 1967. Cf. also Lewis, and Patterson.
[60] Cf. Rodney, pp.103ff.
[61] Cf. Beaud, pp.41f., following Marx's analysis.
[62] See on Hobbes Macpherson.
[63] See on Locke *ibid.* and Beaud, pp.33ff.
[64] Cf. Locke, chapter 5.

[65] Cf. Duchrow, 1991, pp.30ff.

[66] Locke, pp.293ff. and Binswanger, 1982, pp.97ff.

[67] Cf. Binswanger, 1982, pp.102ff. and 110ff.

[68] Cf. *ibid.*, 116ff.

[69] Cf. Binswanger, 1985.

[70] See W. Carey, pp. (67ff.) 81ff. However, he says that mission should neither use violence nor make a profit, thus showing its good intentions, without realizing the implications of the structural link between trade and missionary endeavour.

[71] For this text I thank Aleida Assman, Heidelberg.

[72] Galeano, pp.218f. The analogous example of the Jesuit missions in China under Ricci, and in India under Nobili are omitted here for reasons of space.

[73] Cf. Chaney, pp.9ff.

[74] Williams, 1971, pp.255ff.

[75] My thanks to Aleida Assmann for pointing out this poem.

[76] Williams, 1964, p.105.

[77] *Ibid.*, pp.102ff.

[78] Beaud (pp.64ff.) gives a concise but good overview.

[79] On the following see K. Polanyi, pp.37ff.

[80] Cf. Beaud, pp.72f., 125ff., and Duchrow, 1991, p.36.

[81] Binswanger, 1985.

[82] Cf. Duchrow, 1991, p.32.

[83] Polanyi, pp.78f.

[84] Cf. Binswanger, 1985 and 1990, pp.197-223.

[85] Hinkelammert, 1986.

[86] Galeano, pp.198ff.; cf. also Beaud, pp.115ff.

[87] Cf. Kennedy, pp.29ff.

[88] Galeano, p.221.

[89] Cf. *ibid.*, pp.205 and 228ff.

[90] I shall not go into this question, which is often discussed and fills volumes, and just direct the reader to the concise treatment of it in Beaud, pp.102ff.

[91] Cf. Duchrow, 1991, pp.40f.

[92] Kupisch, pp.68ff., summarizes this period indicating further literature.

[93] See *ibid.* pp.80ff.

[94] Cf. Duchrow, 1987, chapter 1.

[95] See Kupisch, p.104.

[96] *Ibid.*, pp.105ff.

[97] Cf. the overview in Heyer, pp.135ff.

[98] Cf. Gern.

[99] Fabri.

[100] *Ibid.*, p.101; cf. Gern, p.153.

[101] Cf. *ibid.*, p.158ff.

[102] Pannikar, 1955, pp.406ff.

[103] Beaud, p.141.
[104] *Ibid.*, p.144.
[105] Cf. also Kennedy, pp.301ff.
[106] Beaud, p.146.
[107] *Ibid.*, p.148.
[108] Cf. *ibid.*, p.156, and Hirsch, 1986 and 1990.
[109] Cf. Granados/Gurgsdies, p.160.
[110] *Ibid.*, p.165ff.
[111] Cf. Nair/Opperskalski.
[112] Chomsky, p.48.
[113] Cf. Dussel, pp.62-101.
[114] R. van Drimmelen gives an overview of official statements by ecumenical assemblies on the question of economic justice.
[115] Hirsch, 1990, p.104, referring back to Hirsch/Roth, pp.78ff.
[116] Fröbel/Heinrichs/Kreye, 1986.
[117] Hirsch, 1990, p.105.
[118] Cf. WEN, 1988 and 1990.
[119] From an article in *Frankfurter Rundschau*, 25.7.91.
[120] Hirsch, 1990, p.107.
[121] Cf. Hirsch, p.107.
[122] Cf. Duchrow, 1991.
[123] From the abundant literature cf. especially Potter, Vallely, George.
[124] This reads like a detective novel in Greider.
[125] Cf. Potter, pp.97ff.
[126] Budhoo.
[127] Cf. Clairemonte, 1989.
[128] Frank, 1988, pp.33ff.
[129] Cf. in detail Duchrow/Eisenbürger/Hippler.
[130] Cf. *ibid.*, pp.246ff.
[131] Hippler, 1992.
[132] See *New York Times*, 8 March 1992.
[133] Duchrow/Eisenbürger/Hippler.
[134] Cf. WCC/Seoul, and Kinnamon.
[135] One exception has been the Commission on the Churches' Participation in Development (CCPD). See the publication "Economics–A Matter of Faith".
[136] Kinnamon, p.76.
[137] There are two excellent new studies explicating this argument from a socio-economic and a scientific ecological point of view; R. Kurz, and L. Mayer.
[138] Cf. Dussel, pp.62-101.
[139] Hirsch, 1990, p.125.
[140] Cf. Duchrow, 1987, pp.150ff.
[141] Hirsch, 1990.

Notes 97

[142] *Ibid.*, pp.32f.
[143] *Ibid.*, p.34.
[144] *Ibid.*, p.36.

Part II

[1] Cecchini report.
[2] This is the title of Galtung.
[3] WEN, 1988 and 1990; Boerma; Deppe *et al.* (ed.); Kessler; Heine *et al.* (ed.).
[4] Taken from Heine, p.17.
[5] Its 16 volumes are summarized in a short report "The European Challenge, 1992". The study had only a limited task, that of demonstrating the economic costs of not realizing the Single Market, but it has been enlisted again and again as a confirmation of it.
[6] Cf. Duchrow, 1991, pp.32ff.
[7] Heine, p.21.
[8] Cf. Kessler, p.15.
[9] Cf. Goldberg, in Deppe, pp.69ff.
[10] Cf. Clairemonte, 1989.
[11] Heine.
[12] Cf. Duchrow, 1987, pp.150ff.
[13] Heine, p.13.
[14] See Metzger in Heine, pp.77ff.
[15] Cf. S. George.
[16] See pp.27f. above.
[17] Cf. Budhoo.
[18] Cf. Hinkelammert, 1991.
[19] Metzger in Heine, p.78.
[20] *Ibid.*, p.79.
[21] Cf. especially Götzmann and Seifert in Heine, pp.41ff.
[22] *EC Magazine*, 5, 1989, p.5.
[23] From Heine, p.47.
[24] *Ibid.*, p.55.
[25] *Frankfurter Rundschau*, 16 July 1991.
[26] *Ibid.*
[27] Cf. Nübel in Heine, pp.133ff.
[28] In BUKO-Agrokoordination (ed.), pp.343ff. Its authors are: Workgroup on Farming (ABL); Federal Congress of World Development Groups (BUKO), Agrokoordination; German Federation for the Environment and the Protection of Nature (BUND); consumer initiatives. The "Development NGO GATT Steering Committee" (Ave. Cortenbergh 62, B-1040 Brussels) is working along the same lines on a European basis.
[29] Cf. Boerma, and *Faith in the City*.
[30] Cf. WEN, 1988 and 1990; Goldberg in Deppe, pp.83ff.; Reis/Wienand; Hölscher/Beckann *et al.* in Heine, pp.25ff. and 115ff.
[31] Cf. especially Hölscher in Heine, pp.25ff.

[32] Reprint in Reis/Wienand, pp.421ff.

[33] In Heine, p.127.

[34] *Ibid.*

[35] *Ibid.*, p.130.

[36] Cf. Springe, pp.22ff. on the Christian position on the 1989 draft of the Social Charter.

[37] Cf. the basic studies of Schunter-Kleeman, 1990 (ed.) and 1991; see also Eiermacher in Deppe, pp.148ff. In February 1990 the Ecumenical Forum of Christian Women in Europe wrote a letter to Jacques Delors, President of the EC Commission, with an urgent plea for measures to combat the increasingly strong discrimination against women in Europe.

[38] Cf. Schunter-Kleemann, 1991, p.83.

[39] *Ibid.*, pp.84ff.

[40] It is not only the British government that has constantly tried to sabotage European legislation on social matters. The German government, too, made a statement opposing new legislation protecting part-time work, short-term contracts and lease work – affecting particularly women (cf. *Frankfurter Rundschau*, 12 February 1990).

[41] Cf. Niessen in WEN, 1990, pp.16ff. Imbusch offers a detailed analysis of the various groups and the consequences for them of the Single Market.

[42] *Ibid.*, pp.41ff.

[43] *Ibid.*, p.14.

[44] *Ibid.*, pp.26f.

[45] Cf. Cruz.

[46] *Ibid.*, pp.3f.

[47] Cf. Cruz, pp.5f.

[48] Cf. Imbusch, pp.8f., and George, pp.110ff.

[49] Cf. Kasper/Schikora in Heine, pp.95ff., and Hey in Deppe, pp.165ff.

[50] For the interconnectedness of the liberation of creation, justice and peace in the biblical concept of shalom see Duchrow/Liedke, pp.47ff. and 145ff.

[51] Cf. Klass, p.126.

[52] See Frank, 1991.

[53] Duchrow/Eisenbürger/Hippler, p.55.

[54] Cf. Hippler.

[55] Cf. Böge in Deppe, pp.236ff.

[56] See Duchrow/Eisenbürger/Hippler, pp.33ff. and 189ff.

[57] From BurgerInnen kontrollieren die Polizei *et al.*, p.4.

[58] From Renner, p.129. Cf. "A Churches' Guide to European Institutions", issued by the Ecumenical Centre in Brussels.

[59] For the following see Sühlo and Raulfs in Heine, pp.195ff.

[60] *Ibid.*, p.199.

[61] Cf. Hamelink, 1991, and the "Lima Declaration".

Part III

[1] Cf. de Santa Ana.

[2] Frei Betto, in epd-Entwicklungspolitik 16/90, p.d.

[3] Gorastiaga, p.7.

⁴ De Pury.

⁵ I have taken this from an unpublished manuscript with the title "Personal and Public".

⁶ There are also remarkable examples of decentralized financial systems serving Microenterprises; see Malkamäki.

⁷ Cf. de Santa Ana, and Hirsch, 1990.

⁸ Information on this can be obtained from the European Coordination Office, c/o Theo Kneifel, Hegenichstr. 22, 6900 Heidelberg, Germany.

⁹ See CCPD/WCC, 1991.

¹⁰ Contact address: Gea Boessenkoel, Mariahoek 16-17, 3501 DD Utrecht, The Netherlands.

¹¹ Cf. Unmüßig.

¹² Contact address: Cees Hamelink, International Association for Mass Communication Research, Baden Powellweg 109-111, NL-1069 LD Amsterdam, The Netherlands.

¹³ L. & W. Schottroff, p.71.

¹⁴ Cf. Nogueira.

¹⁵ Cf. Wengst.

¹⁶ See T. Veerkamp.

¹⁷ Cf. Duchrow, 1987, p.176.

¹⁸ Cf. Duchrow/Eisenbürger/Hippler, p.133.

¹⁹ Cf. Lampe, pp.61ff.

²⁰ Cf. Duchrow, 1983, pp.181ff. including a critique of the way in which Augustine unfolds the issue.

²¹ Cf. the journals *Community* and *Sojourners*.

²² I have described the respective attempts from the time of Augustine up to Luther in my book *Christenheit und Weltverantwortung*.

²³ L. & W. Schottroff, pp.49ff.

²⁴ Cf. *ibid.*, pp.63ff.

²⁵ Cf. Duchrow/Liedke, pp.78ff.

²⁶ Cf. Duchrow, 1983, pp.532ff. and 559f.

²⁷ Cf. Huber.

²⁸ Cf. Duchrow, 1991, pp.30ff.

²⁹ Cf. Schottroff, pp.66ff.

³⁰ Bonhoeffer, pp.121ff.

³¹ Tödt in Huber, pp.123ff.

³² Ed. R. MacAfee Brown:.

Bibliography

Armstrong K., *Holy War: The Crusades and Their Impact on Today's World*, New York, Anchor Books, 1992.

Assman, J., *Ma'at. Gerechtigkeit und Unsterblichkeit im Alten Agypten*, Munich, C.H. Beck, 1990.

Bauer, C., "Die Epochen der Papstfinanz", in *Ges. Aufsätze zur Wirtschafts- und Sozialgeschichtew*, Freiburg, Herder, 1965.

Beaud, M., *A History of Capitalism 1500-1980*, London, Macmillan, 1981.

Binswanger, H.-Chr., *Geld und Magie. Deutung und Kritik der modernen Wirtschaft anhand von Goethes Faust*, Stuttgart, Weitbrecht, 1985.

Binswanger, H.-Chr., "Geld und Wirtschaft im Verständnis des Merkantilismus. Zu den Theorien von John Locke (1632-1704) und John Law (1671-1729)", in *Studien zur Entwicklung der ökonomischen Theorie*, II, Berlin, Duncker & Humblot, 1982.

Binswanger, H.-Chr., Faber, M. & Manstetten, R., "The Dilemma of Modern Man and Nature: An Exploration of the Faustian Imperative", in *Ecological Economics*, vol. 2, Amsterdam, International Society for Ecological Economics, 1990.

Boerma, C., *The Poor Side of Europe: The Church and the (New) Poor of Western Europe*, Geneva, WCC, 1989.

Bonhoeffer, D., *Ethics*, London, Collins, 1964.

Budhoo, D., *Enough is Enough. Open Letter of Resignation to the Managing Director of the International Monetary Fund*, New York, New Horizons Press, 1990.

Bürger kontrollieren die Polizei u.a. (Hg.), *Europol: Die Bullen greifen nach den Sternen. Europäische Gemeinschaft der Inneren Sicherheit*, Hamburg, Redaktion Strassenmedizin, 1990.

Carey, W., *An Inquiry into the Obligation of Christians to Use Means for the Conversion of the Heathen*, 1792.

Cecchini report, *The European Challenge 1992: The Benefits of a Single Market*, written by John Robinson, based on the report of the research on "Cost of Non-Europe" steering committee, chairman Paolo Cecchini, Aldershot, UK, Wilwood House, 1988.

Chaney, C.L., *The Birth of Missions in America*, South Pasadena, CA, William Carey Library, 1976.

Chomsky, N., *Turning the Tide*, Boston, South End Press, 1985.

Clairemonte, F.F., "Mechanics of Finance Capital: Merger Mania and Insider Trading", *CCPD Occasional Study Pamphlet*, Geneva, WCC, 1989.

Commission of the European Communities, *Community Charter of the Fundamental Social Rights of Workers*, Luxembourg, Office for Official Publications of the European Communities, 1990.

Commission of the European Communities, *Completing the Internal Market: White Paper from the Commission to the European Council*, Milan, 28-29 June 1985, Brussels, European Community, 1985, COM (85), 310 final.

Bibliography 101

Commission on the Churches' Participation in Development, *1992 — Initiatives*, Geneva, WCC, 1991.

Commission on the Churches' Participation in Development, "Economics: A Matter of Faith", *CCPD Documents: Justice and Development*, No. 11, Geneva, WCC, 1988.

Cruz, A., *Grenzen in Europe – Schengen, Trevi und andere zwischenstaatliche Gremien*, Brussels, Ausschuss der Kirchen für Ausländerfragen in Europa, 1990.

Deppe, F., Huffschmid, J. & Weiner, K.-P. Hg., *1992 — Projekt Europa. Politik und Ökonomie in der Europäischen Gemeinschaft*, Cologne, Pahl-Rugenstein, 1989.

Drimmelen, R. van, "Christian Reflection on Economics", in *Transformation*, vol. 4, nos 3 and 4, Exeter, UK, Paternoster, 1987.

Duchrow, U., *Christenheit und Weltverantwortung*, Stuttgart, Klett-Cotta, 2nd ed. 1983.

Duchrow, U., *Global Economy: A Confessional Issue for the Churches?*, Geneva, WCC, 1987.

Duchrow, U., "Let's Democratise the West as Well", in Archer, K., *Beyond the Death of Socialism*, Occasional Papers no 19, Manchester, William Temple Foundation, 1991.

Duchrow, U., Eisenbürger, G. & Hippler, J., *Total War Against the Poor. Confidential Documents of the 17th Conference of American Armies*, New York, New York Circus Publications, 1990.

Duchrow, U. & Liedke, G., *Shalom: Biblical Perspectives on Creation, Justice and Peace*, Geneva, WCC, 1989.

Dussel, E., "Marx's Economic Manuscripts of 1861-63 and the 'concept' of Dependency", in *Latin American Perspectives*, vol. 17, no. 2, 1990.

Fabri, F., *Bedarf Deutschland der Kolonien?*, Gotha, Friedrich Andreas Perthes, 1879.

Faith in the City, report of the Archbishop of Canterbury's Commission on Urban Priority Areas, London, Church House Publishing, 1985.

Frank, A.G., "American Roulette in the Globonomic Casino: Retrospect and Prospect on the World Economic Crisis Today", in *Research in Political Economy*, vol. 11, 1988.

Frank, A.G., "Der Krieg der Scheinheiligen: Seid verflucht alle beide", in *Blätter für deutsche und internationale Politik*, no. 3, Bonn, Blätter Verlagsgesellschaft mbh, 1991.

Fröbel, F., Heinrichs, J. & Kreye, O., *Die neue internationale Arbeitsteilung. Strukturelle Arbeitslosigkeit in den Industrieländern und die Industrialisierung der Entwicklungsländer*, Reinbek b. Hamburg, Rowohlt, 1977.

Fröbel, F., Heinrichs, J. & Kreye, O., *Umbruch in der Weltwirtschaft. Die globale Strategie: Verbilligung der Arbeitskraft – Flexibilisierung der Arbeit – Neue Technologien*, Reinbek b. Hamburg, Rowohlt, 1986.

Galeano, E., *Die offenen Adern Lateinamerikas. Die Geschichte eines Kontinents*, Wuppertal, Peter Hammer Verlag, 4th ed. 1985 (Spanish: *Las venas abiertas de America Latina*, Montevideo, Universidad de la República, 1971.

Galtung, J., *The European Community: A Superpower in the Making*, London, Allen & Unwin, 1973.

George, S., *The Debt Boomerang: How Third World Debt Harms Us All*, London, Pluto Press, 1992.

Gern, W., "Kolonialismus und Mission in Deutschland zur Zeit Bismarcks", in *Theologische Brosamen für Lothar Steiger*, Heidelberg, University of Heidelberg, 1985.

Gorastiaga, X., "The Church of the Poor", in *Latinamerica Press*, vol. 22, no. 27, 1990 (also in *CCPD for Change*, no. 4, 1990).

Granados, G. & Gurgsdies, E., *Lern- und Arbeitsbuch Ökonomie. Eine Einführung in die*

Probleme der westdeutschen Wirtschaftsentwicklung, Bonn, Verlag Neue Gesellschaft, 1985, 3rd ed.

Gross, B., *Friendly Fascism: The New Face of Power in America*, Boston, South End Press, 1980.

Gutiérrez, G. *Gott oder das Gold. Der befreiende Weg des Bartholomé de Las Casas*, Freiburg, Herder, 1990 (Spanish: *Dios o el oro en las Indias. Siglo XVI*, Lima, Instituto Bartolomé de las Casas, 1989).

Hamelink, C. "Media Magnates Are Turning Their Backs on Freedom of the Press", in *Global Affairs*, Amsterdam, Society for International Development/SID, 10 May 1991.

Heine, M., Kisker, K.P. & Schikora, A. Hg., *Schwarzbuch EG-Binnenmarkt. Die vergessenen Kosten der Integration*, Berlin, Sigma, 1991.

Heyer, F., *Die katholische Kirche von 1648 bis 1870 (Die Kirche in ihrer Geschichte*, vol. 4, section N), Göttingen, Vandenhoeck & Ruprecht, 1963.

Hill, C., *The Century of Revolution, 1604-1714*, London, Nelson, 1961.

Hill, C., *Reformation to Industrial Revolution: The Pelican Economic History of Britain*, vol. 2, 1530-1780, Harmondsworth, UK, Penguin Books, 2nd ed. 1969.

Hinkelammert, F.J., "Die Einsamkeit der Dritten Welt", in *Lateinamerika Tage 1991*, 13-23 June 1991, Berlin, FDCL, 1991.

Hinkelammert, F.J., *The Ideological Weapons of Death: A Theological Critique of Capitalism*, Maryknoll, NY, Orbis, 1986.

Hippler, J., *The New World Order*, London, Pluto Press, 1992.

Hirsch, J., *Kapitalismus ohne Alternative? Materialistische Gesellschaftstheorie und Möglichkeiten einer sozialistischen Politik heute*, Hamburg, VSA-Verlag, 1990.

Hirsch J. & Roth, R., *Das neue Gesicht des Kapitalismus. Vom Fordismus zum Postfordismus*, Hamburg, VSA-Verlag, 1986.

Hobbes, T., *Leviathan*, Harmondsworth, UK, Penguin Classics (1st ed. 1651), 1986.

Huber, W. Hg., *Protestanten in der Demokratie. Positionen und Profile im Nachkriegsdeutschland*, Munich, Kaiser, 1990.

Imbusch, P., *1992. Die Folgen der Vollendung des EG-Binnenmarktes für europäische und aussereuropäische Migranten*, Marburg, Forschungsgruppe Europäische Gemeinschaften, 1991.

Kennedy, P., *The Rise and Fall of the Great Powers: Economic Change and Military Conflict from 1500 to 2000*, London, Fontana, 5th printing 1990.

Kessler, W., *Europäischer Binnenmarkt – Vision oder Alptraum*, Oberursel, Publik-Forum, 1989.

Kinnamon, M. ed., *Signs of the Spirit*, report of the WCC's seventh assembly, Canberra, 1991, Geneva, WCC, 1991.

Klass, J., *EG-Binnenmarkt und Entwicklungsländer. Bausteine für Unterricht und Bildungsarbeit*, 1990.

Kupisch, K., *Deutschland im 19. und 20. Jahrhundert (Die Kirche in ihrer Geschichte*, vol. 4, section R), Göttingen, Vandenhoeck & Ruprecht, 1966.

Kurz, R., *Der Kollaps der Modernisierung. Vom Zusammenbruch des Kasernensozialismus zur Krise der Weltökonomie*, Frankfurt, Eichborn, 1991.

Lape, P., "Die Apokalyptiker – ihre Situation und ihr Handeln", in *Eschatologie und Frieden*, vol. II, Heidelberg, Protestant Institute for Interdisciplinary Research/FEST, 1978.

Las Casas, B. de, *Bericht von der Verwüstung der westindischen Länder*, ed. H.M. Enzensberger, Frankfurt, Insel, 1981.

Lewis, G.K., *Slavery, Imperialism and Freedom. Studies in English Radical Thought*, New York/London, Monthly Review Press, 1978.

Lima Declaration, *Towards a New Communication (1990)*, in *EPD-Entwicklungspolitik*, 10/11, Frankfurt, Evang. Pressedienst/EPD, May 1991.

Locke, J., *Two Treatises of Government* (1690), ed. P. Laslett, Cambridge, Cambridge University Press, 1988.

Lüthi, H., "Variationen über ein Thema von Max Weber. Die Protestantische Ethik und der Geist des Kapitalismus", in Lüthi, H., *Zur Gegenwart der Geschichte*, Cologne/Berlin, Kiepenheuer & Witsch, 1967.

MacAfee Brown, R. ed., *Kairos – Three Prophetic Challenges to the Church*, Grand Rapids, MI, Eerdmans, 1990.

MacPherson, C.B., *The Political Theory of Possessive Individualism. Hobbes to Locke*, Oxford, Oxford University Press, 1962.

Malkamäki, M., *Banking the Poor. Informal and Semi-formal Financial Systems Serving the Microenterprises*, University of Helsinki, Institute of Development Studies, 1991.

Mayer, L., *Ein System siegt sich zu Tode. Der Kapitalismus frisst seine Kinder*, Frankfurt, Publik-Forum, 1992.

Meueler, E. Hg., *Unterentwicklung. Arbeistmaterialien für Schüler, Lehrer und Aktionsgruppen*, vol. 1, Reinbek b. Hamburg, Rowohlt, 1974.

Mires, F., *Im Namen des Kreuzes. Ger Genozid an den Indianern während der spanischen Eroberung: theologische und politische Diskussionen*, Fribourg/Brig, Exodus, 1989.

Nair, K. & Opperskalski, M., *CIA: Club der Mörder. Der US-Geheimdienst in der Dritten Welt*, Göttingen, Lamuv, 1988.

Nogueira, P.A. de Souza, *Der Widerstand gegen Rom in der Apokalypse des Johannes – Eine Untersuchung zur Tradition des Falls von Babylon in Apokalypse 18*, Heidelberg, dissertation, manuscript, 1991.

Panikkar, K.M., *Asia and the Dominion of the West*, Zurich, 1955.

Patterson, O., *Sociology of Slavery: An Analysis of the Origins, Development and Structure of Negro Slave Society in Jamaica*, Cranbury, NJ, USA, Fairleigh Dickinson, 1970.

Polanyi, K., *Origins of Our Time: The Great Transformation*, London, Gollancz, 1945.

Potter, G.A., *Dialogue on Debt: Alternative Analyses and Solutions*, Washington, DC, Center of Concern, 1988.

Pury, Pascal de, *People's Technologies and People's Participation*, Geneva, WCC/CCPD, 1983.

Reis, C. & Wienand, M., *Zur sozialen Dimension des EG-Binnenmarktes, Texte u. Materialien 2*, Frankfurt, Eigenverlag des Deutschen Vereins für öffentl. und private Fürsorge, 1990.

Renner, G., *1000 Chancen -- 1000 Risiken. Binnenmarkt '92*, Bühl/Baden, 1990.

Santa Ana, J. de, Raiser, K. & Duchrow, U., *The Political Economy of the Holy Spirit*, Geneva, WCC, 1990.

Schottroff, L. & Schottroff, W., "Biblische Traditionen von 'Staatstheologie, Kirchentheologie und Prophetischer Theologie' nach dem Kairos-Dokument", in Shottroff, L. & Shottroff, W., *Die Macht der Auferstehung*, Sozialgeschichtliche Bibelauslegungen, Munich, Kaiser, 1988.

Schunter-Kleemann, S., "EG-Binnenmarkt – Markt der Möglichkeiten oder Markt der Betrogenen", in *Beiträge zur feministischen Theorie und Praxis*, no. 29, 1991.

Schunter-Kleemann, S. Hg., "EG-Binnenmarkt-Europatriarchat oder Aufbruch der Frauen?",

Schriftenreihe der wissenschaftl. Einheit Frauenstudien und Frauenforschung an der Hochschule, vol. 2, Bremen, University of Bremen, 1990.

Springe, Chr., "Ein soziales Europa oder ein Europa der Starken?", Bremen, Junge Kirche, 1990.

Todorov, T., *Die Eroberung Amerikas. Das Problem des Anderen*, Frankfurt, Suhrkamp, 1985.

Unmüssig, B., "Brückenforum in Bonn-Beuel: Auf dem Weg zu neuen Allianzen?" in *Informationsbrief Weltwirtschaft und Entwicklung*, Königswinter, WEED, July 1991.

Vallely, P., *Bad Samaritans: First World Ethics and Third World Debt*, London, Hodder & Stoughton, 1990.

Veerkamp, T., "Die Priester, der Büttel und der Narr. Auslegung von Joh. 18,28-19,16", in *Texte und Kontexte*, no. 41, Berlin, Lehrhaus, e.v., April 1989.

Wallerstein, I., *The Modern World-System: Capitalist Agriculture and the Origins of the European World-Economy in the Sixteenth Century*, New York, Academic Press, 1974.

Wengst, K., *Pax Romana. Anspruch und Wirklichkeit. Erfahrungen und Wahrnehmungen des Friedens bei Jesus und im Urchristentum*, Munich, Kaiser, 1985.

WEN (West European Network "Work, Unemployment and the Churches"), *The Other Side of 1992*, Manchester, William Temple Foundation, 1990.

WEN (West European Network "Work, Unemployment and the Churches"), *Poverty and Polarisation: A Call to Commitment*, Manchester, William Temple Foundation, 1988.

Williams, Eric, *Capitalism and Slavery*, London, André Deutsch, 2nd ed. 1964.

Williams, Eric, *From Columbus to Castro: The History of the Caribbean 1492-1969*, New York, Random, 1983.

World Council of Churches, final texts from the world convocation on "Justice, Peace and the Integrity of Creation", Seoul 1990, Geneva, WCC, 1990.

Zinn, K.G., *Kanonen und Pest. Uber die Ursprünge der Neuzeit im 14. und 15. Jahrhundert*, Opladen, Westdeutscher Verlag, 1989.